Fix Your Laser Printer and Save a Bundle

Fix Your Laser Printer and Save a Bundle

Paul Lapsansky

iUniverse, Inc.
New York Lincoln Shanghai

Fix Your Laser Printer and Save a Bundle

Copyright © 2005 by Paul Lapsansky

iUniverse books may be ordered through booksellers or by contacting:

iUniverse
2021 Pine Lake Road, Suite 100
Lincoln, NE 68512
www.iuniverse.com
1-800-Authors (1-800-288-4677)

ISBN: 0-595-34305-8

Printed in the United States of America

CONTENTS

INTRODUCTION

This book has been compiled from technical bulletins, manufacturer's service manuals, third party parts and service provider documents as well as my own accumulation of over ten years of knowledge in servicing laser printers. Unlike other maintenance and repair books that offer more theory and less specific troubleshooting, this book covers specific problems and solutions I have encountered while servicing laser printers from Hewlett-Packard, Apple, IBM/Lexmark and Panasonic.

How exactly does this book differ from a service manual?

This book is intended to be a supplement to and not a replacement for a service manual. It assumes that you have proficient knowledge in the field of electronics including the use of tools and diagnostic aids as well as soldering and desoldering. While service manuals provide helpful information such as schematics, parts lists and assembly and disassembly instructions, they are specific to a certain model and don't offer the years of field experience in troubleshooting and repair found in this book as well as sources for parts.

How do I use this book?

Each chapter is broken down by either manufacturer or "engine". An "engine" as it applies to laser printers refers to the mechanism the printer uses to create the laser output. Many different makes and models of laser printers are based on the same printer "engine" and so share common parts as well as problems and solutions. Each chapter describes common problems along with suggested solutions. If you don't see a problem that matches one you are looking for, than you can refer to the list of error codes and their meaning as well as common defects and their causes.

Why should I repair?

This question comes up quite frequently and with good reason given that laser printers are now available for under $500. But, before you decide to discard that old printer, remember parts for older laser printers are often less costly and the output from many older models is quite comparable to many newer models. Also, many of the "under $500" models are designed for light usage or "duty cycle" and so are not as rugged as some older models. If you do decide to repair than using this book just one time can easily pay for itself in time and money saved. Even if you choose to have your printer repaired professionally instead of repairing it yourself, this book can still help you avoid costly and unnecessary repairs.

CHAPTER 1

Standard 300 DPI Workgroup Printers

SX Engine
HP LaserJet II/IID/III/IIID
Apple LaserWriter II Series

IBM/Lexmark
4019/4028/4029/4039/4049

Panasonic
KX-P4410/P4420/P4430/P4450/P4450I/P4455

Problem: Makes groaning noise as paper exits output tray.

Model(s): All SX engine printers

Diagnosis: This is usually the result of worn delivery rollers.

Solution: Replace delivery rollers.

Problem: Chirping noise emanating from back of printer while unit is printing.

Model(s): All SX engine printers

Diagnosis: This is usually the result of worn bearings in the upper cooling fan.

Solution: Replace upper cooling fan.

Problem: Chirping noise emanating from back of printer even when unit is idle.

Model(s): All SX engine printers

Diagnosis: This is usually the result of worn bearings in the lower cooling fan.

Solution: Replace lower cooling fan.

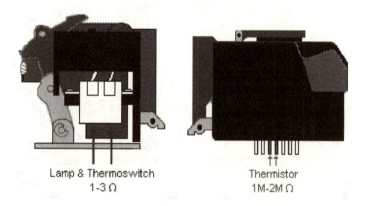

Lamp & Thermoswitch
1-3 Ω

Thermistor
1M-2M Ω

Figure 1-1

Problem: Both Red LED's Flashing.

Model(s): Apple LaserWriter II

Diagnosis: This error indicates that the fuser has failed to reach or maintain a proper temperature. Nine times out of ten, the problem lies with either the fusing assembly or the AC power module, which supplies power to the fuser. The quartz lamp inside the fuser often fails. This lamp can be replaced individually, but it is often best to replace the entire fuser.

Solution: 1). Remove fuser assembly and do a resistance check (see Figure 1-1), replace if defective. 2). Replace AC power module. 3). Check cable running from J200 on DC controller to fuser assembly. 4). Check for +24V from DC power supply and replace if necessary.

Problem: Steady Red Right LED (Paper Jam).

Model(s): Apple LaserWriter II

Diagnosis: Usually the result of worn gears or rollers. Most of the time it is caused by a worn pickup roller as this roller is made of rubber and begins to dry out or harden over time and use. Gears inside the fuser assembly also wear with time and heat. When this occurs, the delivery rollers will fail to turn properly resulting in a paper jam. Another overlooked cause is the main motor drive gears. The grease applied to these gears often hardens with time and temperature and will begin to bind if not properly lubricated.

Solution: 1). If paper jam occurs before paper leaves tray, check or replace pickup assembly and separation pad. 2). If paper jam occurs at registration, check or replace registration assembly. 3). If paper jam occurs at fuser, check or replace fuser assembly. Also, check main motor drive gears. 4). If paper jam occurs past fuser assembly, check or replace delivery rollers. Also, check 14-tooth gear and 20-tooth gear for wear on fuser assembly.

Problem: Intermittent distorted image down page.

Model(s): HP LaserJet II and III

Diagnosis: This problem is often the result of damage to internal cables or loose connections.

Solution: Check cable between DC controller and HV power supply.

Problem: Black smudges at the top of the backside of the first page out and toner buildup around Transfer Corona.

Model(s): HP LaserJet II and III

Diagnosis: This problem is often the result of damage to internal cables or loose connections.

Solution: Check cable between DC controller and HV power supply.

Problem: Intermittent 41, 51 or 52 Error.

Model(s): HP LaserJet II, III, IID and IIID

Diagnosis: This problem is often the result of damage to internal cables or loose connections.

Solution: 1). Check cables between DC controller and laser scanner. 2). Inspect fiber optic cable. 3). Replace laser scanner. 4). Replace DC controller.

Problem: 50 Service Error.

Model(s): HP LaserJet II, III, IID and IIID

Diagnosis: This error indicates that the fuser has failed to reach or maintain a proper temperature. Nine times out of ten, the problem lies with either the fusing assembly or the AC power module, which supplies power to the fuser. The quartz lamp inside the fuser often fails. This lamp can be replaced individually, but it is often best to replace the entire fuser.

Solution: 1). Remove fuser assembly and do a resistance check (see Figure 1-1), replace if defective. 2). Replace AC power module. 3). Check cable running from J200 on DC controller to fuser. 4). Check for +24V from DC power supply and replace if necessary.

Problem: Intermittent 50 Service Error (not solved by previous 50 Service solution).

Model(s): HP LaserJet II, III, IID and IIID

Diagnosis: This problem is often the result of damage to internal cables or loose connections.

Solution: Inspect cable running from thermistor/exit PCA to DC controller.

Problem: Intermittent 55 error and/or 12 Printer Open and/or missing print and/or smeared print.

Model(s): HP LaserJet II, III, IID and IIID

Diagnosis: A clogged ozone filter or failing upper cooling fan can cause excessive draw on the DC power supply resulting in various problems.

Solution: Replace ozone filter and replace if necessary, upper cooling fan.

Problem: 13 Paper Jam.

Model(s): HP LaserJet II, III, IID, and IIID

Diagnosis: Usually the result of worn gears or rollers. Most of the time it is caused by a worn pickup roller as this roller is made of rubber and begins to dry out or harden over time and use. Gears inside the fuser assembly also wear with time and heat. When this occurs, the delivery rollers will fail to turn properly resulting in a paper jam. Another overlooked cause is the main motor drive gears. The grease applied to these gears often hardens with time and temperature and will begin to bind if not properly lubricated.

Solution: 1). If paper jam occurs before paper leaves tray, check or replace pickup assembly and separation pad. 2). If paper jam occurs at registration, check or replace registration assembly. 3). If paper jam occurs at fuser, check or replace fuser assembly. Also, check main motor drive gears. 4). If paper jam occurs past fuser assembly, check or replace delivery rollers. Also, check 14-tooth gear and 20-tooth gear for wear on fuser assembly.

Problem: Light print, eventually leading to a 16 Toner Low message even with a new cartridge installed.

Model(s): HP LaserJet IID & IIID

Diagnosis: Adjusting toner density dial yields little improvement. Probable suspect is the DC controller.

Solution: Replace DC controller.

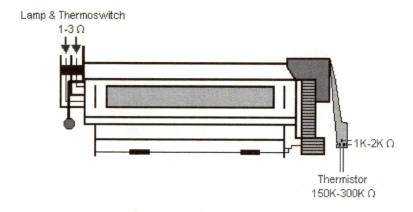

Figure 1-2

Problem: 9-2 Error.

Model(s): IBM/Lexmark 4019

Diagnosis: This error indicates that the fuser has failed to reach or maintain a proper temperature.

Solution: 1). Inspect thermistor cable. 2). Remove fuser assembly and do a resistance check (see Figure 1-2), replace if necessary. 3). Replace LVPS.

Problem: 920, 921, 922 or 923 Error.

Model(s): IBM/Lexmark 4029

Diagnosis: This error indicates that the fuser has failed to reach or maintain a proper temperature.

Solution: 1). Inspect thermistor cable. 2). Remove fuser assembly and do a resistance check (see Figure 1-2), replace if necessary. 3). Replace LVPS.

Problem: Paper feed errors.

Model(s): IBM/Lexmark 4019/4029

Diagnosis: Usually the result of worn D-roll.

Solution: Inspect D-roll and replace if necessary.

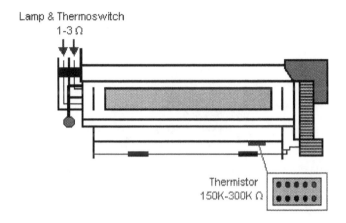

Figure 1-3

Problem: 920, 921, 922 or 923 Error.

Model(s): IBM/Lexmark 4039/4049

Diagnosis: This error indicates that the fuser has failed to reach or maintain a proper temperature.

Solution: 1). Inspect thermistor cable. 2). Remove fuser assembly and do a resistance check (see Figure 1-3), replace if necessary. 3). Replace LVPS.

Problem: Paper feed errors.

Model(s): IBM/Lexmark 4039/4049

Diagnosis: Usually the result of worn D-roll.

Solution: Inspect D-roll and replace if necessary.

Problem: Call Service E13.

Model(s): KX-P 4450 and P4450i

Diagnosis: This error indicates a problem with toner density. Before troubleshooting, make sure the correct toner is being used. In addition, high and low humidity can cause this error. If these check out, the problem most likely lies with the developer unit.

Solution: 1). Inspect and replace if necessary developer unit. 2). Inspect hopper, hopper motor and drive PCB. 3). Inspect developer connectors on main logic board. 4. Replace main logic board.

Problem: Call Service E35.

Model(s): KX-P4410, P4420, P4430, P4450, and P4450i

Diagnosis: This error indicates that the laser unit has failed.

Solution: 1). Inspect connection between laser unit and main logic board. 2). Replace laser unit. 3). Replace main logic board.

Problem: Call Service E36, E37 or E38.

Model(s): KX-P4450

Diagnosis: This error indicates that the laser unit has failed.

Solution: 1). Inspect connection between laser unit and main logic board. 2). Replace laser unit. 3). Replace main logic board.

Problem: E62, blank display, UNDEF TRAP PLEASE TURN OFF message, excessive toner dumping.

Model(s): KX-P4410, P4430, P4440, and P5410

Diagnosis: This error usually occurs after having disassembled the printer and is most likely the result of a pair of springs that attach to the transfer corona not being reinstalled properly.

Solution: Verify springs attached to transfer corona are installed properly.

Problem: Call Service E31.

Model(s): KX-P4420

Diagnosis: This error indicates that the fuser has failed to reach or maintain a proper temperature.

Solution: 1). Inspect all connections on main motor PCB. 2). Perform resistance check on fuser (lamp resistance should be about 2½ ±1 and thermistor is about 100k½ ±20k). 3). Verify that fuser is receiving 115 VAC (if not inspect connectors and if necessary, replace power supply). 4). Replace main logic board.

CHAPTER 2

Standard 600+ DPI Workgroup Printers

EX Engine
HP LaserJet 4/4M/4 Plus/4M Plus
HP LaserJet 5/5M/5N
Apple LaserWriter Pro

52X Engine
HP LaserJet 4000/4050

Problem: False paper jams instead of paper out message.

Model(s): All EX engine printers

Diagnosis: This is usually the result of a missing or damaged paper out sensor flag, which is often lost or damaged during paper installation.

Solution: Inspect and replace if missing or damaged, paper sensor flag (RB1-2133).

Problem: 13 Paper Jam Error (sometimes 41.3).

Model(s): HP LaserJet 4/4M

Diagnosis: This problem is usually caused by poor quality paper. If problem persists, HP has introduced a modified corner tab for the 250-sheet paper tray.

Solution: Install redesigned corner tab.

Problem: 57 Error.

Model(s): HP LaserJet 4/4M

Diagnosis: This error is usually caused by a defective main motor.

Solution: Replace main motor.

Problem: 13 Paper Jam Error (paper folded like accordion as it leaves fuser assembly).

Model(s): HP LaserJet 4/4M

Diagnosis: This problem was a result of a number of printers being manufactured with a defective output roller holder. It is best to replace the entire paper output assembly.

Solution: Replace paper output assembly.

Problem: False 14 No EP Cart error.

Model(s): HP LaserJet 4/4M/4Plus/4MPlus

Diagnosis: This is often caused by replacing the toner cartridge without shutting off the printer. Although HP does not advise to, it is best to shut off the printer when changing cartridge.

Solution: 1). Reseat toner cartridge. 2). Check toner cartridge contacts. 3). Swap out toner cartridge. 4). Replace high voltage power supply.

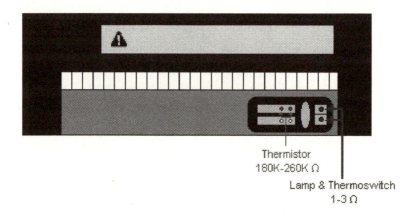

Thermistor
180K-260K Ω

Lamp & Thermoswitch
1-3 Ω

Figure 2-1

Problem: 50 Service Error.

Model(s): HP LaserJet 4/4M/4Plus/4MPlus/5/5M/5N

Diagnosis: This error indicates that the fuser has failed to reach or maintain a proper temperature.

Solution: 1). Remove fuser assembly and do a resistance check (see Figure 2-1), replace if defective. 2). Replace power supply. 3). Check cable from fuser to DC controller and power supply. 4). Check cable from power supply to DC controller. 5). Replace DC controller.

Problem: Repeated disassembly due to paper jam.

Model(s): HP LaserJet 4000

Diagnosis: HP has addressed this problem with a revised Tray 1 pickup assembly and registration assembly. Both help make it easier to remove paper jams with having to disassembly.

Solution: Install upgrade from HP, Tray 1 Pickup Assembly (RG5-2655) and Registration Assembly (RG5-2652).

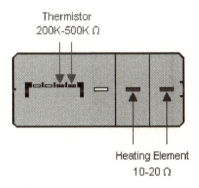

Figure 2-2

Problem: 50.x Fuser Error.

Model(s): HP LaserJet 4000 and 4050

Diagnosis: This error indicates that the fuser has failed to reach or maintain a proper temperature.

Solution: 1). Remove fuser assembly and do a resistance check (see Figure 2-2), replace if defective. 2). Replace engine control board.

Problem: Paper not grabbing from one of the paper trays (not 500 Sheet option).

Model(s): HP LaserJet 4000 and 4050

Diagnosis: Though this problem is often caused by worn feed separation rollers, it can also be caused by a missing or damaged pickup coupler. The pickup coupler sits between the pickup rollers and drive mechanism. It is often damaged when the paper tray is overfilled. If the pickup rollers fail to turn than suspect the pickup coupler.

Solution: 1). Inspect and replace if necessary, feed separation rollers. 2). If feed separation rollers are not turning, replace pickup coupler.

Problem: Image skewing or damage when paper fed from 250-sheet tray.

Model(s): All EX engine printers

Diagnosis: This is usually the result of a missing paperweight above the 250-sheet paper tray.

Solution: Remove 250-sheet paper tray and look for "V" shaped hinged weight hanging down. Replace weight if missing (front—RF5-0369 and back—RB1-2259).

Problem: Spontaneous engine print test generation.

Model(s): 4000 and 4050

Diagnosis: Dirty or defective engine test switch.

Solution: Clean engine test switch. Replace engine control board.

CHAPTER 3

Personal and Small Workgroup Printers

LX Engine
HP LaserJet IIp/IIp Plus/IIIp
Apple Personal LaserWriter

PX Engine
HP LaserJet 4L/4ML/4P/4MP

AX Engine
HP LaserJet 5L/6L/3100/3150

22X Engine
HP LaserJet 1100/3200

VX Engine
HP LaserJet 5P/5MP/6P/6MP

Problem: Paper Jam when exiting upper tray. Paper usually scrunches up like an "accordion".

Model(s): All LX engine printers

Diagnosis: This is usually caused by worn delivery rollers.

Solution: Replace delivery rollers.

Problem: Paper Jam before paper reaches toner cartridge. Paper usually scrunches up like an "accordion".

Model(s): All LX engine printers

Diagnosis: This is caused by a failed EP drum drive assembly. This part drives the drum inside the toner cartridge. When it fails, the drums will not turn resulting in the paper jam.

Solution: Replace EP drum drive assembly.

Problem: Paper Jam, will not grab paper from multi-purpose tray.

Model(s): All LX engine printers

Diagnosis: This is usually the result of worn pickup rollers. The rollers are made of rubber, which eventually dries or hardens with use and age.

Solution: Replace paper pickup rollers and separation pad.

Problem: "Moan" sound during paper pick-up.

Model(s): All LX engine printers

Diagnosis: This problem is often caused by a spring on the bottom of the separation pad. It appears that the spring is too long. A revised separation pad has been made available. The type and weight of paper is used can also be the cause.

Solution: Replace separation pad with updated pads.

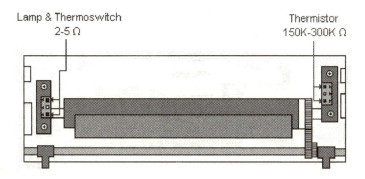

Figure 3-1

Problem: 50 Service Error.

Model(s): HP LaserJet IIP, IIP Plus and IIIP

Diagnosis: This error indicates that the fuser has failed to reach or maintain a proper temperature. It is most often the result of a blown quartz lamp in the fuser. Although the quartz lamp can be replaced individually, it is often best to replace the entire fuser assembly.

Solution: 1). Remove fuser assembly and do a resistance check (see Figure 3-1), replace if defective. 2). Check for continuity between cables from fuser to DC controller and from power supply to fuser. 3). Replace power supply. 4). Replace DC controller.

Problem: Flashing Red and Yellow Lights.

Model(s): Apple Personal LaserWriter NT/NTR/SC

Diagnosis: This message indicates a fuser or laser scanner malfunction. Visually check to see if quartz lamp in fuser illuminates. If not than it is probably a fuser related problem. If error occurs while trying to print (usually accompanied by high pitch wine), than it is probably a laser scanner related problem.

Solution: For fuser related problem: 1). Remove fuser assembly and do a resistance check (see Figure 3-1), replace if defective. 2). Check for continuity between cables from fuser to DC controller and from power supply to fuser. 3). Replace power supply. 4). Replace DC controller. For laser scanner related problem: 1). Replace scanner motor.

Problem: Intermittent 41 Error progressing to solid 52 or sometimes 51 Error.

Model(s): HP LaserJet IIP, IIP Plus and IIIP

Diagnosis: This error is most often caused by a failing scanner motor. It should be noted that on early model IIP's, static charge build up on the fuser could cause intermittent 41 Errors. This was corrected by replacing the fuser with an updated "three diode" fuser.

Solution: Replace scanner motor. Replace "two diode" fuser with "three diode" fuser if applicable.

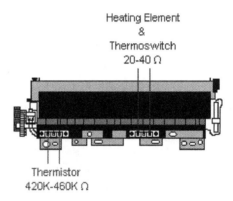

Figure 3-2

Problem: All four LEDs on, Ready and Error LEDs light when front panel button is pressed.

Model(s): HP LaserJet 4L/4ML

Diagnosis: This error indicates that the fuser has failed to reach or maintain a proper temperature.

Solution: 1). Remove fuser assembly and do a resistance check (see Figure 3-2), replace if defective. 2). Swap out DC controller.

Problem: Constant Paper Jams.

Model(s): HP LaserJet 4L/4ML/4P/4MP

Diagnosis: This is most often caused by damage to the paper input sensor flag during paper jam removal. If the sensor becomes damaged, than the printer will be inoperable.

Note: The revised sensor arm may come into contact with the high voltage shield. If this is the case, replace high voltage shield with modified high voltage shield.

Solution: Inspect and replace if damaged, paper input sensor flag with re-designed paper input sensor flag and if necessary, high voltage shield.

Note: The revised sensor arm may come into contact with the high voltage shield. If this is the case, replace high voltage shield with modified high voltage shield.

Problem: Frequent paper jams and image skewing.

Model(s): HP LaserJet 4L/4ML/4P/4MP

Diagnosis: This is usually the result of a damaged paper cassette from excessive pushing down or pulling up on the cassette subsequently resulting in damaged support guides.

Solution: Replace paper cassette or install paper cassette support guide repair kit (5062-4662).

Problem: 50 Service Error.

Model(s): HP LaserJet 4P/4MP

Diagnosis: This error indicates that the fuser has failed to reach or maintain a proper temperature.

Solution: 1). Remove fuser assembly and do a resistance check (see Figure 3-2), replace if defective. 2). Swap out DC controller.

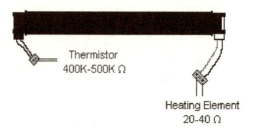

Figure 3-3

Problem: All three LEDs on, Error and Ready LEDs light when front panel button is pressed.

Model(s): All AX engine printers

Diagnosis: This error indicates that the fuser has failed to reach or maintain a proper temperature. This printer uses a ceramic heating element instead of the conventional lamp fuser.

Solution: 1). Remove fuser assembly and do a resistance check (see Figure 3-3), replace if defective. 2). Swap out DC controller.

Problem: Paper Jam when exiting fuser. Paper usually scrunches up like an "accordion".

Model(s): HP LaserJet 5L

Diagnosis: This often results in the printer having to be disassembled to remove paper jam from fuser area. HP as added an output bin to help alleviate this problem.

Solution: Install output bin (RB1-7332).

Problem: Feeds multiple pages at a time or will not pickup paper at all.

Model(s): All AX engine printers

Diagnosis: This is a common problem with Canon AX "gravity feed" printers and is most often due to worn pickup roller and separation pads. It will often start out with the printer grabbing multiple pages at a time and eventually progress to not picking up paper at all.

Solution: Replace paper pickup assembly and separation pad and sub pads.

Problem: All three LEDs on, Go and Ready LEDs light when front panel button is pressed.

Model(s): HP LaserJet 1100

Diagnosis: This error indicates that the fuser has failed to reach or maintain a proper temperature. This printer uses a ceramic heating element instead of the conventional lamp fuser.

Solution: 1). Remove fuser assembly and do a resistance check (see Figure 3-3), replace if defective. 2). Swap out DC controller.

Problem: Feeds multiple pages at a time or will not pickup paper at all.

Model(s): HP LaserJet 1100

Diagnosis: This is similar to a common problem with Canon AX printers and is due to worn pickup roller and separation pads. It will often start out with the printer grabbing multiple pages at a time and eventually progress to not picking up paper at all.

Solution: Replace paper pickup roller and separation pad and sub pads.

Problem: First four LEDs lit. Paper Jam LED lights when Go and Rest/Job Cancel are held down.

Model(s): HP LaserJet 5P/5MP/6P/6MP

Diagnosis: This error indicates that the fuser has failed to reach or maintain a proper temperature.

Solution: 1). Remove fuser assembly and do a resistance check (see Figure 3-2), replace if defective. 2). Swap out DC controller.

CHAPTER 4

High-Volume Printers

NX Engine
HP LaserJet IIISi
HP LaserJet 4Si/4Si MX

WX Engine
HP LaserJet 5Si/5Si Mopier/5Si MX/5Si NX
HP LaserJet 8000

Problem: Intermittent 13.1 or 13.2 error.

Model(s): All NX engine printers

Diagnosis: If the printer fails to grab paper than it is most likely pickup rollers. If the jam occurs before the fuser than it is probably a problem with the fuser assembly sensor arm.

Solution: 1). Inspect and replace if necessary, pickup/separation rollers. 2). Inspect and replace if necessary fuser assembly sensor arm. If fuser is worn, replace entire fuser assembly.

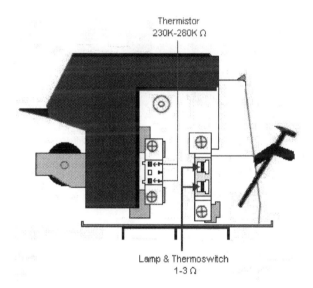

Figure 4-1

Problem: 50 Service Error.

Model(s): All NX engine printers

Diagnosis: This error indicates that the fuser has failed to reach or maintain a proper temperature.

Solution: 1). Remove fuser and do resistance check (see Figure 4-1), replace if defective. 2). Replace AC power supply. 3). Replace sensor PCA. 4). Inspect cable from DC controller. 5). Replace DC controller.

Problem: Intermittent missing scan lines from top of page.

Model(s): HP LaserJet 4Si/4Si MX

Diagnosis: This is usually caused from the bumper mounted on the job offset assembly becoming deformed and causing the assembly to "bang" when it moves left and vibrate the beam-to-drum mirror.

Solution: Replace job offset assembly.

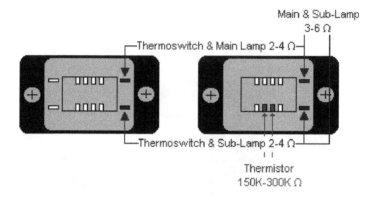

Figure 4-2

Problem: 50.x Fuser Error.

Model(s): All WX engine printers

Diagnosis: This error indicates that the fuser has failed to reach or maintain a proper temperature.

Solution: 1). Remove fuser and do resistance check (see Figure 4-2), replace if defective. 2). Inspect cable from DC controller. 3). Replace DC controller.

Problem: 13.2 Paper Jam Error from all trays.

Model(s): All WX engine printers

Diagnosis: This error indicates that the printer did not detect paper arriving at the registration in time. Since it is occurring from all trays, suspect a registration problem.

Solution: Inspect and replace if necessary registration assembly and sensor.

Problem: 13.2 Paper Jam Error (sometime 58.3 error) from Tray 1 only.

Model(s): All WX engine printers

Diagnosis: This error indicates that the printer did not detect paper arriving at the registration in time. Since it does not occur with the other trays, suspect a problem with Tray 1.

Solution: 1). Inspect and replace if necessary Tray 1 paper pickup roller and separation pad. 2). If paper fails to lift, replace Tray 1 pickup assembly with improved unit.

Problem: 13.1 or 13.2 Paper Jam Error from Tray 2, 3 or 4.

Model(s): All WX engine printers

Diagnosis: A 13.1 Paper Jam Error indicates that the printer did not detect paper arriving at the paper input unit (PIU) in time. A 13.2 Paper Jam Error indicates that the printer did not detect paper arriving at the registration in time.

Solution: 1). Check paper stock (avoid using higher than #24). 2). Check tray paper size adjustment. 3). Swap paper tray. 4). Inspect and replace if necessary paper pickup and fee/separation rollers. 5). Check registration assembly. 6). Replace paper input unit (PIU).

Problem: "False" 13.14 Paper Jam Error.

Model(s): HP LaserJet 5Si/5Si MX/5Si NX

Diagnosis: This error is often caused by a flag on the face down delivery assembly resulting in a "false" paper jam message.

Solution: Check face down delivery sensor.

Problem: 13.2 Paper Jam Error from Tray 3.

Model(s): HP LaserJet 5Si/5Si MX/5Si NX

Diagnosis: This error indicates that the printer did not detect paper arriving at the registration in time. Since it does not occur with the other trays, suspect a problem with Tray 3.

Solution: Replace Second Pass Roller Assembly (RB1-6581) or recommend replacing entire paper pickup assembly (RG5-1852).

Problem: 43 Error listed in error log but does not show on display.

Model(s): HP LaserJet 5Si/5Si MX/5Si NX

Diagnosis: This usually indicates a problem with the memory SIMMs on the formatter. If memory was recently installed, insure that it is of correct type.

Solution: Check and/or replace SIMM(s).

Problem: Repetitive print problems (ghosting) due to toner build up on fuser pressure roller.

Model(s): HP LaserJet 5Si/5Si MX/5Si NX

Diagnosis: HP has addressed this issue by adding a cleaning roller to the fuser assembly to reduce toner buildup. This upgrade is already built into the 8000 fuser.

Solution: Install fuser upgrade kit or replace fuser assembly with updated fuser.

Problem: Fan #3 noisy.

Model(s): HP LaserJet 5Si/5Si MX/5Si NX

Diagnosis: This is caused by excessive fan vibration in some models.

Solution: Install noise kit (5182-5899).

Problem: 79 Service Errors with sub-codes 81EE, 8101, 0101, 0142 or 8108.

Model(s): HP LaserJet 5Si/5Si MX/5Si NX

Diagnosis: These errors are common to the original firmware revision 7.9. Verify firmware version (found on configuration page).

Solution: Replace formatter PCB with formatter PCB with updated firmware if revision is 7.9.

Problem: 70 Service Errors

Model(s): HP LaserJet 5Si/5Si MX/5Si NX

Diagnosis: This error can be caused by a faulty 16MB (revision "B") SIMMs manufactured by HP. Faulty SIMMs can be identified the identification number "HM5117400BS6" on them.

Solution: Verify whether the revision "B" SIMM is installed. Replace with non-revision "B" SIMM if necessary.

Problem: 13.2 Paper Jams or 41.3 Wrong Paper Size Errors when printing from Tray 1.

Model(s): HP LaserJet 5Si/5Si MX/5Si NX

Diagnosis: If pick-up roller fails to turn, than suspect a defective clutch.

Solution: Replace Tray 1 pick-up assembly (RG5-1880).

Problem: 20 Memory Overflow error sometimes followed by 79 Service (40E0).

Model(s): HP LaserJet 5Si/5Si MX/5Si NX

Diagnosis: This problem is common to the original firmware revision 7.9. Verify firmware version (found on configuration page).

Solution: Replace formatter PCB with formatter PCB with updated firmware if revision is 7.9.

Problem: Repeated paper jams while feeding from the 2,000-Sheet Feeder.

Model(s): HP LaserJet 5Si/5Si MX/5Si NX

Diagnosis: This is often caused by were to the right cover which causes paper to stick to the paper guide.

Solution: Inspect and if necessary install sixteen rib right cover assembly (RG5-1519).

Problem: Smeared print.

Model(s): HP LaserJet 5Si/5Si MX/5Si NX

Diagnosis: Some models are vulnerable to smeared print, the result of a coating on the transfer roller and current applied to the roller.

Solution: Replace transfer roller and DC controller with updated unit (RG5-1844).

Problem: Problem with toner adhesion when printing from trays 2 or 3.

Model(s): HP LaserJet 5Si/5Si MX/5Si NX

Diagnosis: This problem can occur if the DC controller has firmware revision 1.11 or in some cases, 2.22. To determine which firmware version your DC controller has, verify the number on IC201 on the DC controller. If it a "02", than it is revision 1.11, if it is a "05" than it is revision 2.22 and if it is a "060", than it is revision 2.6.

Solution: Replace DC controller if firmware is revision 2.22 or less.

Problem: Printer sometimes hangs while printing from power save mode after a power cycle reset.

Model(s): HP LaserJet 5Si/5Si MX/5Si NX

Diagnosis: This problem is common to the original firmware revision 7.9. Verify firmware version (found on configuration page).

Solution: Replace formatter PCB with formatter PCB with updated firmware if revision is 7.9.

Problem: Internal trays do not lift while in "POWERSAVE" mode.

Model(s): HP LaserJet 5Si/5Si MX/5Si NX

Diagnosis: This problem occurs when one of the internal trays is opened while the printer is in "POWERSAVE" mode. This problem has been address with firmware version 9.1. Verify firmware version (found on configuration page).

Solution: Replace formatter PCB with formatter PCB with firmware 9.1 or higher if necessary.

Problem: Toner dumping sometimes accompanied by 79 Service w/(04CC) sub-code.

Model(s): HP LaserJet 5Si/5Si MX/5Si NX

Diagnosis: Make sure problem is not the result of a failed toner cartridge. If not, than this problem can occur if the DC controller has firmware revision 1.11. To determine which firmware version your DC controller has, verify the number on IC201 on the DC controller. If it a "02", than it is revision 1.11, if it is a "05" than it is revision 2.22 and if it is a "060", than it is revision 2.6.

Solution: Replace DC controller if the firmware is revision 1.1.

Problem: Printer sometimes hangs while printing a PostScript configuration page if "TRAY 2 EMPTY" is displayed on the front panel.

Model(s): HP LaserJet 5Si/5Si MX/5Si NX

Diagnosis: This problem is common to the original firmware revision 7.9. Verify firmware version (found on configuration page).

Solution: Replace formatter PCB with formatter PCB with updated firmware if revision is 7.9.

Problem: Printer sometimes hangs displaying "PROCESSING JOB".

Model(s): HP LaserJet 5Si/5Si MX/5Si NX

Diagnosis: This problem has been address with firmware version 9.1. Verify firmware version (found on configuration page).

Solution: Replace formatter PCB with formatter PCB with updated firmware.

Problem: Intermittent MIO and NVRAM reset after printer is turned off and then back on again.

Model(s): HP LaserJet 5Si/5Si MX/5Si NX

Diagnosis: This problem has been address with firmware version 8.6. Verify firmware version (found on configuration page).

Solution: Replace formatter PCB with formatter PCB with firmware 8.6 or higher if necessary.

Problem: 13.3 Paper Jam Error from Tray 3.

Model(s): HP LaserJet 8000

Diagnosis: This error indicates that the printer did not detect paper arriving at the registration in time. Since it does not occur with the other trays, suspect a problem with Tray 3.

Solution: Replace Second Pass Roller Assembly (RB1-6581) or recommend replacing entire paper pickup assembly (RG5-1852).

Problem: 55 Error

Model(s): All NX engine printers

Diagnosis: Defective DC power supply.

Solution: Replace DC power supply.

Problem: 55.3 or 55.A Error

Model(s): All WX engine printers

Diagnosis: Incompatibility between duplexer and fuser.

Solution: Replace fuser assembly and/or duplexer.

CHAPTER 5

Large Format Printers

BX Engine
HP LaserJet 4V/4MV

62X Engine
HP LaserJet 5000

Problem: 57.1 Service Error.

Model(s): HP LaserJet 4V/4MV

Diagnosis: This error normally indicates a main motor failure but can also be the result of a broken spring in the front door open sensor.

Solution: Inspect spring (RS5-2125) and replace if necessary else replace main motor assembly.

Problem: 67 Service Errors.

Model(s): HP LaserJet 4V/4MV

Diagnosis: Defective paper guide plate assembly.

Solution: Replace paper guide plate assembly (RG5-2248).

Problem: Jams from optional 500 Sheet tray.

Model(s): HP LaserJet 4V/4MV

Diagnosis: This issue has been addressed by HP with a revised roller and clip kit.

Solution: Install revised roller and clip.

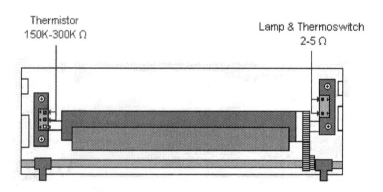

Figure 5-1

Problem: 50 Service Error.

Model(s): HP LaserJet 4V/4MV

Diagnosis: This error indicates that the fuser has failed to reach or maintain a proper temperature.

Solution: Remove fuser assembly and do a resistance check (see Figure 5-1).

Problem: 55 Service Error.

Model(s): HP LaserJet 4V/4MV

Diagnosis: This problem is usually the result of a communication error between the DC controller and the formatter PCA and is often caused by

Solution: Reseat the formatter PCA.

Problem: Smudge on leading edge of paper.

Model(s): HP LaserJet 4V/4MV

Diagnosis: Toner can build up on edge of fuser entrance guide.

Solution: Replace fuser assembly with revised fuser.

Problem: Paper Jams when printing to three-hole punched paper.

Model(s): HP LaserJet 4V/4MV

Diagnosis: The DC controller on some printers may not allow enough time for the paper to pass the first paper sensor.

Solution: Install revised DC controller PCA.

Problem: Paper Jams when feeding from MP Tray.

Model(s): HP LaserJet 4V/4MV

Diagnosis: Some early units experienced frequent paper jamming when printing from MP Tray due to static charge eliminator and guide assembly.

Solution: Install revised static charge eliminator (RB1-5467) and revised guide assembly (RG5-1555).

Problem: MP Tray pick-up roller does not stop.

Model(s): HP LaserJet 4V/4MV

Diagnosis: On occasion the pick-up clutch will not disengage resulting in continued paper pick-up from the MP Tray and eventual paper jam.

Solution: Replace paper guide plate assembly.

Problem: Paper jams at output with large media.

Model(s): HP LaserJet 4V/4MV

Diagnosis: Toner build up on the face down delivery rollers.

Solution: Clean or replace face down delivery assembly rollers.

Problem: Cannot access service mode.

Model(s): HP LaserJet 4V/4MV

Diagnosis: Some printers may have firmware that will not detect depressed control panel keys during power-up.

Solution: Install patch SIMM (C3141-60003) or replace formatter PCA with updated formatter.

Problem: Noisy formatter fan sometimes with 58.3 Error.

Model(s): HP LaserJet 4V/4MV

Diagnosis: This problem is usually the resulting of a failing upper or formatter fan or cable.

Solution: Inspect cable between fan and DC controller. Replace fan if necessary.

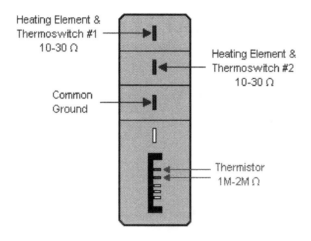

Figure 5-2

Problem: 50.x Fuser Error.

Model(s): HP LaserJet 5000

Diagnosis: This error indicates that the fuser has failed to reach or maintain a proper temperature.

Solution: 1). Remove fuser assembly and do a resistance check (see Figure 5-2) and replace if defective. 2). Replace DC controller.

CHAPTER 6

Common Visual Defects

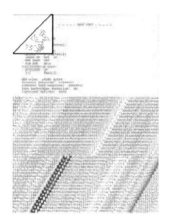

Problem: Back of page dirty.

Model(s): All SX engine printers

Diagnosis: 1). Toner cartridge leaking. 2). Dirty cleaning wand. 3). Defective HV power supply cable to DC controller.

Solution: 1). Inspect toner cartridge and replace if leaking. 2). Inspect cleaning wand and replace if dirty. 3). Inspect HV power supply cable to DC controller.

Model(s): HP LaserJet 4000/4050

Diagnosis: 1). Inside of printer dirty. 2). Dirty pickup roller. 3). Dirty transfer roller. 4). Dirty fuser assembly.

Solution: 1). Clean paper path and check for toner leaks (print cleaning page). 2). Clean or replace pickup roller. 3). Clean or replace transfer roller. 4). Clean or replace fuser assembly.

Model(s): All LX engine printers

Diagnosis: 1). Toner cartridge leaking. 2). Transfer roller dirty. 3). Input feed roller dirty. 4). Toner build-up in fuser.

Solution: 1). Inspect toner cartridge and replace if leaking. 2). Clean or replace transfer roller. 3). Clean or replace input feed roller. 4). Clean fuser assembly (use cleaning page from self-test page).

Model(s): All AX engine printers

Diagnosis: 1). Inside of printer dirty. 2). Dirty pickup roller. 3). Dirty transfer roller. 4). Dirty heating element or pressure roller.

Solution: 1). Clean paper path and check for toner leaks. 2). Clean or replace pickup roller. 3). Clean or replace transfer roller. 4). Clean heating element and pressure roller.

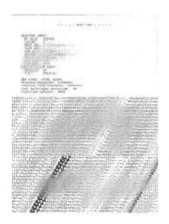

Problem: Toner smear (poor fusing).

Model(s): All SX engine printers

Diagnosis: 1). Paper out of spec. 2). Defective toner cartridge. 3). Dirty fuser cleaning wand. 4). Defective fuser assembly. 5). Defective static eliminator teeth.

Solution: 1). Try different paper. 2). Inspect toner cartridge and replace if necessary. 3). Inspect cleaning wand and replace if necessary. 4). Inspect fuser assembly and replace if necessary. 5). Inspect static eliminator teeth and replace transfer corona assembly if defective.

Model(s): All EX engine printers

Diagnosis: 1). Paper out of spec. 2). Static eliminator teeth dirty or defective. 3). Dirty or defective fuser. 4). Worn gears in toner cartridge.

Solution: 1). Try different paper. 2). Clean or replace static eliminator assembly. 3). Clean or replace fuser assembly. 4). Replace toner cartridge.

Model(s): HP LaserJet 4000/4050

Diagnosis: 1). Paper too smooth. 2). Defective fuser.

Solution: 1). Check paper type. 2). Replace fuser assembly.

Model(s): All LX engine printers

Diagnosis: 1). Print density improperly set. 2). Paper or media out of spec. 3). Defective fuser. 4). Defective HV power supply. 5). Defective DC controller.

Solution: 1). Try increasing density. 2). Try different paper or media. 3). Replace fuser assembly. 4). Replace HV power supply. 5). Replace DC controller.

Model(s): All PX/VX engine printers

Diagnosis: 1). Paper out of spec. 2). Static eliminator teeth dirty or defective. 3). Dirty or defective fuser. 4). Defective DC controller.

Solution: 1). Try different paper. 2). Clean or replace static eliminator assembly. 3). Clean or replace fuser assembly. 4). Replace DC controller.

Model(s): All AX engine printers and LaserJet 1100

Diagnosis: 1). Toner density setting needs adjustment. 2). Paper out of spec. 3). Dirty HV contact points. 4). Defective toner cartridge. 5). Defective transfer roller. 6). Defective heating element or pressure roller. 7). Defective DC controller.

Solution: 1). Adjust toner density setting through software. 2). Try different paper. 3). Inspect toner cartridge and replace if necessary. 4). Clean HV contact points on toner cartridge and on transfer roller. 5). Replace transfer roller. 6). Inspect and replace if necessary, heating element or pressure roller. 7). Replace DC controller.

Model(s): All NX engine printers

Diagnosis: 1). Paper out of spec. 2). Static eliminator teeth dirty or defective. 3). Dirty or defective fuser.

Solution: 1). Try different paper. 2). Clean or replace static eliminator assembly. 3). Clean or replace fuser assembly.

Model(s): All WX engine printers

Diagnosis: 1). Paper out of spec. 2). Static eliminator teeth dirty or defective. 3). Dirty or defective fuser. 4). Defective DC controller.

Solution: 1). Try different paper. 2). Clean or replace static eliminator. 3). Clean or replace fuser assembly. 4). Replace DC controller.

Model(s): All BX engine printers

Diagnosis: 1). Print density improperly set. 2). Paper or media out of spec. 3). Defective fuser. 4). Defective HV power supply. 5). Defective DC controller.

Solution: 1). Try increasing density. 2). Try different paper or media. 3). Replace fuser assembly. 4). Replace HV power supply. 5). Replace DC controller.

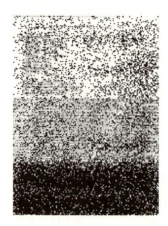

Problem: Sued print.

Model(s): All SX engine printers

Diagnosis: 1). Defective DC controller. 2). Defective formatter PCA.

Solution: Perform test print from DC controller. If sued print occurs, replace DC controller. If defect does not occur with DC controller test print than replace formatter PCA.

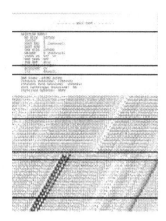

Problem: Horizontal black lines.

Model(s): All SX engine printers

Diagnosis: 1). Defective fiber optic cable. 2). Defective laser/scanner. 3). Defective DC controller.

Solution: 1). Inspect fiber optic cable and replace if necessary. 2). Replace laser/scanner assembly. 3). Replace DC controller.

Model(s): IBM/Lexmark 4019/4029

Diagnosis: 1). Toner cartridge defective or improperly installed. 2). Print head shutter not functioning properly. 3). Defective HVPS cable. 4). Poor transfer corona contacts.

Solution: 1). Reseat toner cartridge or replace if necessary. 2). Inspect print head shutter. 3). Inspect HVPS cable and check for proper continuity, replace if necessary. 4). Clean and inspect transfer corona contacts. 5). Replace system board.

Model(s): IBM/Lexmark 4039/4049

Diagnosis: 1). Toner cartridge defective or improperly installed. 2). Print head shutter not functioning properly. 3). Defective HVPS cable. 4). Poor transfer roller contacts.

Solution: 1). Reseat toner cartridge or replace if necessary. 2). Inspect print head shutter. 3). Inspect HVPS cable and check for proper continuity, replace if necessary. 4). Clean and inspect transfer roller contacts.

Model(s): All EX engine printers

Diagnosis: 1). Defective laser/scanner assembly. 2). Defective DC controller.

Solution: 1). Replace laser/scanner assembly. 2). Replace DC controller.

Model(s): HP LaserJet 4000/4050

Diagnosis: 1). Poor connections on laser/scanner and engine controller. 2). Defective laser/scanner. 3). Defective engine controller.

Solution: 1). Reseat connectors on laser/scanner and engine controller. 2). Replace laser/scanner assembly. 3). Replace engine controller board.

Model(s): All PX/VX engine printers

Diagnosis: 1). Toner cartridge not installed properly. 2). Defective toner cartridge. 3). See repetitive defect.

Solution: 1). Reinstall toner cartridge. 2). Inspect toner cartridge and replace if necessary.

Model(s): All AX engine printers and LaserJet 1100

Diagnosis: 1). Toner cartridge not installed properly. 2). Defective toner cartridge. 3). Paper path dirty. 4). Defective heating element or pressure roller.

Solution: 1). Reinstall toner cartridge. 2). Inspect toner cartridge and replace if necessary. 3). Clean paper path. 4). Inspect and replace if necessary, heating element or pressure roller.

Model(s): All NX engine printers

Diagnosis: 1). Defective fiber-optic cable. 2). Defective laser/scanner. 3). Defective DC controller.

Solution: 1). Inspect fiber-optic cable and replace if necessary. 2). Replace laser/scanner assembly. 3). Replace DC controller.

Problem: Faulty registration.

Model(s): All SX engine printers

Diagnosis: 1). Paper out of spec. 2). Worn paper pickup roller. 3). Defective registration assembly. 4). Dirty or worn drive gears. 5). Defective paper tray.

Solution: 1). Try different paper. 2). Inspect paper pickup roller and replace if necessary. 3). Replace registration assembly. 4). Clean and lubricate drive gears, replace if worn. 5). Replace paper tray.

Model(s): All EX engine printers

Diagnosis: 1). Paper out of spec. 2). Worn paper feed rollers. 3). Defective input/registration sensor. 4). Worn or defective drive gear. 5). Defective paper tray. 6). Defective DC controller.

Solution: 1). Try different paper. 2). Inspect and replace if necessary, pickup and separation rollers. 3). Replace input/registration sensor. 4). Inspect and replace if necessary, drive gears and main drive assembly. 5). Inspect paper tray and replace if necessary. 6). Replace DC controller.

Model(s): All LX engine printers

Diagnosis: 1). Paper out of spec. 2). Worn paper pickup rollers and separation pad. 3). Registration needs adjustment. 4). Drive gears are worn. 5). Defective paper input sensor.

Solution: 1). Try different paper. 2). Inspect paper feed roller assembly and separation pad and replace if necessary. 3). Adjust registration via VR201 on

DC controller. 4). Inspect drive gears and replace if necessary. 5). Inspect paper input sensor and replace if necessary.

Model(s): All PX/VX engine printers

Diagnosis: 1). Paper out of spec. 2). Worn paper feed rollers. 3). Registration out of adjustment. 4). Worn or defective drive gears. 5). Paper cassette paper guide out of adjustment.

Solution: 1). Try different paper. 2). Inspect and replace if necessary, pickup and separation rollers. 3). Adjust registration. 4). Inspect and replace if necessary, drive gears and main drive assembly. 5). Adjust paper guide to correct paper size.

Model(s): All AX engine printers

Diagnosis: Registration adjustment required.

Solution: Adjust VR202 on DC controller.

Model(s): All NX engine printers

Diagnosis: 1). Paper out of spec. 2). Worn paper feed rollers. 3). Defective registration assembly. 4). Worn or defective drive gear. 5). Defective paper tray.

Solution: 1). Try different paper. 2). Inspect and replace if necessary, pickup and separation rollers. 3). Inspect and replace if necessary, registration assembly. 4). Inspect and replace if necessary, drive gears and main drive assembly. 5). Inspect paper tray and replace if necessary.

Model(s): All WX engine printers

Diagnosis: 1). Paper guide incorrectly adjusted. 2). Paper out of spec. 3). Worn or defective drive gear. 4). Worn pickup or registration rollers.

Solution: 1). Adjust paper guide. 2). Try different paper. 3). Inspect and replace if necessary, drive gears and main drive assembly. 4). Inspect and replace if necessary, pickup and registration rollers.

Model(s): All BX engine printers

Diagnosis: 1). Paper out of spec. 2). Worn paper pickup rollers. 3). Dirty or worn drive gears.

Solution: 1). Try different paper. 2). Inspect paper pickup roller assembly and replace if necessary. 3). Clean and lubricate drive gears, replace if worn.

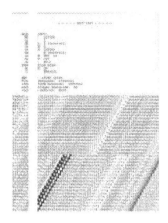

Problem: Right or left hand text missing or distorted.

Model(s): All SX engine printers

Diagnosis: 1). Low toner. 2). Beam-to-drum mirror out of alignment. 3). Defective top cover hinge bracket.

Solution: 1). Shake toner cartridge to redistribute toner or replace cartridge. 2). Verify beam-to-drum mirror is aligned correctly. 3). Replace top cover hinge bracket.

Problem: Vertical white streaks.

Model(s): All SX engine printers

Diagnosis: 1). Dirty beam-to-drum mirror. 2). Dirty transfer corona wire. 3). Defective toner cartridge. 4). Defective laser/scanner.

Solution: 1). Clean beam-to-drum mirror. 2). Clean or replace transfer corona wire. 3). Replace toner cartridge. 4). Replace laser/scanner assembly.

Model(s): All EX engine printers

Diagnosis: 1). Low toner. 2). Defective laser/scanner.

Solution: 1). Shake toner cartridge to redistribute toner or replace cartridge. 2). Replace laser/scanner assembly.

Model(s): HP LaserJet 4000/4050

Diagnosis: 1). Low toner or defective cartridge. 2). Dirty paper path. 3). Defective fuser. 4). Defective laser/scanner.

Solution: 1). Inspect toner cartridge and replace if necessary. 2). Clean printer paper path. 3). Replace fuser assembly. 4). Replace laser/scanner assembly.

Model(s): All PX/VX engine printers

Diagnosis: 1). Low toner. 2). Dirty beam-to-drum mirror. 3). Defective laser/scanner.

Solution: 1). Shake toner cartridge to redistribute toner or replace cartridge. 2). Clean beam-to-drum mirror. 3). Replace laser/scanner assembly.

Model(s): All AX engine printers

Diagnosis: 1). Toner cartridge getting low. 2). Inside of printer dirty.

Solution: 1). Shake toner cartridge to redistribute toner. Replace toner cartridge if necessary. 2). Clean paper path.

Model(s): All NX engine printers

Diagnosis: 1). Low toner. 2). Dirty beam-to-drum mirror. 3). Defective laser/scanner.

Solution: 1). Shake toner cartridge to redistribute toner or replace cartridge. 2). Clean beam-to-drum mirror. 3). Replace laser/scanner assembly.

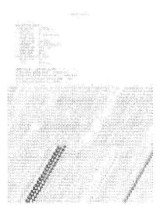

Problem: Faint print.

Model(s): All SX engine printers

Diagnosis: 1). Low toner. 2). Paper out of spec. 3). Dirty or defective drum ground contacts. 4). Defective transfer corona. 5). Dirty or defective HV power supply cable.

Solution: 1). Shake toner cartridge to redistribute toner or replace cartridge. 2). Try different paper. 3). Inspect drum ground contacts and clean or replace if necessary. 4). Replace transfer corona assembly. 5). Inspect HV power supply cable and clean or replace if necessary. 6). Replace high voltage power supply.

Model(s): IBM/Lexmark 4019/4029

Diagnosis: 1). Low toner. 2). Print darkness setting set too low. 3). Print head shutter not functioning properly. 4). Defective HVPS cable. 5). Defective transfer corona.

Solution: 1). Replace toner cartridge if low. 2). Adjust contrast control. 3). Inspect print head shutter. 4). Inspect HVPS cable and check for proper continuity, replace if necessary. 5). Inspect transfer corona and replace if necessary.

Model(s): IBM/Lexmark 4039/4040

Diagnosis: 1). Low toner. 2). Print darkness setting set too low. 3). Print head shutter not functioning properly. 4). Defective HVPS cable. 5). Poor transfer roller contacts.

Solution: 1). Replace toner cartridge if low. 2). Set print darkness on the customer menu to Normal or Dark. 3). Inspect print head shutter. 4). Inspect

HVPS cable and check for proper continuity, replace if necessary. 5). Clean and inspect transfer roller contacts.

Model(s): All EX engine printers

Diagnosis: 1). Low toner. 2). Print density setting set too low. 3). EconoMode enabled. 4). Paper out of spec. 5). Defective transfer roller.

Solution: 1). Shake toner cartridge to redistribute toner or replace cartridge. 2). Set density to darker setting. 3). Disable EconoMode. 4). Try different paper. 5). Replace transfer roller.

Model(s): HP LaserJet 4000/4050

Diagnosis: 1). Toner cartridge getting low. 2). Toner density setting needs adjustment. 3). EconoMode enabled. 4). Defective transfer roller. 5). Dirty contacts on engine controller. 6). Defective laser/scanner. 7). Defective engine controller.

Solution: 1). Shake toner cartridge to redistribute toner. Replace toner cartridge if necessary. 2). Adjust toner density setting through software. 3). Adjust EconoMode setting through software. 4). Replace transfer roller. 5). Clean and inspect contacts on engine controller board. 5). Replace laser/scanner assembly. 6). Replace engine controller board.

Model(s): All LX engine printers

Diagnosis: 1). Low toner. 2). Paper out of spec. 3). Transfer roller defective. 4). HV contact dirty or defective. 5). HV PCA defective. 6). Defective DC controller.

Solution: 1). Shake toner cartridge to redistribute toner or replace cartridge. 2). Try different paper. 3). Replace transfer roller. 4). Clean or replace HV contact assembly. 5). Replace HV PCA. 6). Replace DC controller.

Model(s): All PX/VX engine printers

Diagnosis: 1). Low toner. 2). Print density setting set too low. 3). EconoMode enabled. 4). Paper out of spec. 5). Defective transfer roller. 6). Dirty or defective high voltage connector springs. 7). Laser/scanner shutter door not operating properly. 8). Defective DC controller.

Solution: 1). Shake toner cartridge to redistribute toner or replace cartridge. 2). Set density to darker setting. 3). Disable EconoMode. 4). Try different paper. 5). Replace transfer roller. 6). Inspect high voltage connector springs and clean or replace if necessary. 7). Inspect laser/scanner shutter door and replace laser/scanner assembly if necessary.

Model(s): All AX engine printers and LaserJet 1100

Diagnosis: 1). Toner cartridge getting low. 2. Toner density setting needs adjustment. 3). EconoMode enabled. 4). Dirty HV contact points. 5). Defective laser/scanner. 6). Defective DC controller.

Solution: 1). Shake toner cartridge to redistribute toner. Replace toner cartridge if necessary. 2). Adjust toner density setting through software. 3). Adjust EconoMode setting through software. 4). Clean HV contact points on toner cartridge and on transfer roller. 5). Replace laser/scanner assembly. 6). Replace DC controller.

Model(s): All NX engine printers

Diagnosis: 1). Low toner. 2). Print density setting set too low. 3). Defective drum sensitivity switch. 4). Paper out of spec. 5). Defective transfer roller. 6). Dirty or defective high voltage contact springs. 7). Defective high voltage power supply.

Solution: 1). Shake toner cartridge to redistribute toner or replace cartridge. 2). Set density to darker setting. 3). Inspect drum sensitivity switch. 4). Try different paper. 5). Replace transfer roller. 6). Inspect high voltage connector springs and clean or replace if necessary. 7). Replace high voltage power supply.

Model(s): All WX engine printers

Diagnosis: 1). Low toner. 2). Print density setting set too low. 3). EconoMode enabled. 4). Paper out of spec. 5). Defective transfer roller. 6). Dirty or defective high voltage contact springs. 7). Defective high voltage power supply. 8). Defective DC controller.

Solution: 1). Shake toner cartridge to redistribute toner or replace cartridge. 2). Set density to darker setting. 3). Disable EconoMode. 4). Try different paper. 5). Replace transfer roller. 6). Inspect high voltage connector springs and clean or replace if necessary. 7). Replace high voltage power supply. 8). Replace DC controller.

Model(s): All BX engine printers

Diagnosis: 1). Low toner. 2). Print density setting set too low. 3). EconoMode enabled. 4). Paper out of spec. 5). Transfer roller defective. 6). High Voltage contacts dirty or defective. 7). HV power supply defective. 8). Defective DC controller.

Solution: 1). Shake toner cartridge to redistribute toner or replace cartridge. 2). Set density to darker setting. 3). Disable EconoMode. 4). Try different paper. 5). Replace transfer roller. 6). Clean or replace HV contact assembly. 7). Replace HV power supply. 8). Replace DC controller.

Problem: Black Pages.

Model(s): All SX engine printers

Diagnosis: 1). Defective toner cartridge. 2). Defective laser/scanner cable. 3). Defective laser/scanner. 4). Defective DC controller. 5). Defective formatter PCA.

Solution: 1). Inspect toner cartridge and replace if necessary. 2). Inspect laser/scanner cable and replace if necessary. 3). Replace laser/scanner assembly. 4). Replace DC controller. 5). Replace formatter PCA.

Model(s): IBM/Lexmark 4019/4029

Diagnosis: 1). Dirty or defective HVPS contact springs. 2). Defective HVPS cable. 3). Defective system board.

Solution: 1). Inspect HVPS contact springs and clean or replace if necessary. 2). Inspect HVPS cable and check for proper continuity, replace if necessary. 3). Replace system board.

Model(s): IBM/Lexmark 4039/4049

Diagnosis: 1). Dirty or defective HVPS contact springs. 2). Defective HVPS cable. 3). Defective system board.

Solution: 1). Inspect HVPS contact springs and clean or replace if necessary. 2). Inspect HVPS cable and check for proper continuity, replace if necessary. 3). Replace system board.

Model(s): All EX engine printers

Diagnosis: 1). Defective toner cartridge. 2). Dirty or defective high voltage contact springs. 3). Defective high voltage power supply. 4). Defective DC controller. 5). Defective formatter.

Solution: 1). Inspect toner cartridge and replace if necessary. 2). Inspect high voltage connector springs and clean or replace if necessary. 3). Replace high voltage power supply. 4). Replace DC controller. 5). Replace formatter board.

Model(s): HP LaserJet 4000/4050

Diagnosis: 1). HV power supply connections are dirty. 2). Defective toner cartridge. 3). Defective engine controller board. 4). Defective formatter PCA.

Solution: 1). Clean HV power supply connections and make sure power supply is seated properly. 2). Inspect toner cartridge and replace if necessary. 3). Replace engine controller.

Model(s): All LX engine printers

Diagnosis: 1). Defective toner cartridge. 2). Dirty or defective high voltage contacts. 3). Defective fiber optic cable. 4). Defective high voltage power supply. 5). Defective DC controller. 6). Poor connection between laser/scanner to DC controller. 7). Defect laser/scanner motor.

Solution: 1). Inspect toner cartridge and replace if necessary. 2). Inspect high voltage connectors and clean or replace if necessary. 3). Inspect fiber optic cable and replace if necessary. 4). Replace high voltage power supply. 5). Replace DC controller. 6). Inspect connector and replace if necessary. 7). Replace laser/scanner motor.

Model(s): All PX/VX engine printers

Diagnosis: 1). Defective toner cartridge. 2). Dirty or defective high voltage contact springs. 3). Defective high voltage power supply. 4). Defective DC controller. 5). Poor connection between laser/scanner to DC controller. 6). Defective laser/scanner assembly.

Solution: 1). Inspect toner cartridge and replace if necessary. 2). Inspect high voltage connector springs and clean or replace if necessary. 3). Replace high voltage power supply. 4). Replace DC controller. 5). Inspect connector and replace if necessary. 6). Replace laser/scanner assembly.

Model(s): All AX engine printers and LaserJet 1100

Diagnosis: 1). Toner cartridge installed incorrectly. 2). Toner cartridge defective. 3). Dirty HV contact points. 4). Defective DC controller. 5). Defective laser/scanner.

Solution: 1). Reinstall toner cartridge. 2). Inspect toner cartridge and replace if necessary. 3). Clean HV contact points on toner cartridge and on transfer roller. 4). Replace DC controller. 5). Replace laser/scanner assembly.

Model(s): All NX engine printers

Diagnosis: 1). Defective toner cartridge. 2). Bad laser/scanner assembly cable. 3). Defective laser/scanner. 4). Defective DC controller.

Solution: 1). Replace toner cartridge. 2). Inspect cable and replace if necessary. 3). Replace laser/scanner assembly.

Model(s): All BX engine printers

Diagnosis: 1). Defective toner cartridge. 2). Dirty or defective high voltage contact springs. 3). Defective high voltage power supply. 4). Defective DC controller. 5). Poor connection between laser/scanner to DC controller. 6). Defective laser/scanner assembly.

Solution: 1). Inspect toner cartridge and replace if necessary. 2). Inspect high voltage connector springs and clean or replace if necessary. 3). Replace high voltage power supply. 4). Replace DC controller. 5). Inspect connector and replace if necessary. 6). Replace laser/scanner assembly.

Problem: Smudged horizontal band with overprint.

Model(s): All SX engine printers

Diagnosis: 1). Worn paper pickup roller. 2). Problem with paper drive. 3). Defective toner cartridge.

Solution: 1). Inspect paper feed roller assembly and replace if necessary. 2). Inspect and replace if necessary, paper path drive mechanism, gear train and motor.

Model(s): All LX engine printers

Diagnosis: 1). Worn paper pickup rollers. 2). Drive gears are worn. 3). Defective toner cartridge

Solution: 1). Inspect paper feed roller assembly and replace if necessary. 2). Inspect drive gears and replace if necessary. 3). Replace toner cartridge.

Problem: White or blank pages.

Model(s): All SX engine printers

Diagnosis: 1). Defective toner cartridge. 2). Defective transfer corona wire. 3). Defective HV power supply cable. 4). Defective laser/scanner cable. 5). Defective laser/scanner. 6). Bent top cover hinge brackets.

Solution: 1). Inspect toner cartridge and replace if necessary. 2). Inspect transfer corona wire and replace if necessary. 3). Inspect HV power supply cable and replace if necessary. 4). Inspect laser/scanner cable and replace if necessary. 5). Replace laser/scanner assembly. 6). Inspect top cover hinge brackets and replace if necessary.

Model(s): IBM/Lexmark 4019/4029

Diagnosis: 1). Print head shutter not functioning properly. 2). Defective HVPS cable. 3). Defective transfer corona.

Solution: 1). Inspect print head shutter. 2). Inspect HVPS cable and check for proper continuity, replace if necessary. 3). Inspect transfer corona and replace if necessary. 4). Replace system board.

Model(s): IBM/Lexmark 4039/4049

Diagnosis: 1). Print head shutter not functioning properly. 2). Defective HVPS cable. 3). Poor transfer roller contacts.

Solution: 1). Inspect print head shutter. 2). Inspect HVPS cable and check for proper continuity, replace if necessary. 3). Clean and inspect transfer roller contacts.

Model(s): All EX engine printers

Diagnosis: 1). Empty or defective toner cartridge. 2). Defective transfer roller. 3). Dirty or defective high voltage connector springs. 4). Laser/scanner shutter door not operating properly. 5). Defective high voltage power supply. 6). Defective DC controller. 7). Defective laser/scanner cable.

Solution: 1). Inspect toner cartridge and replace if necessary. 2). Replace transfer roller. 3). Inspect high voltage connector springs and clean or replace if necessary. 4). Inspect laser/scanner shutter door and replace laser/scanner assembly if necessary. 5). Replace high voltage power supply. 6). Replace DC controller.

Model(s): HP LaserJet 4000/4050

Diagnosis: 1). Defective toner cartridge. 2). Defective laser shutter. 3). Damaged toner cartridge guide. 4). HV power supply contacts dirty. 5). Defective transfer roller. 6). Defective engine controller board. 7). Defective laser/scanner cable.

Solution: 1). Inspect toner cartridge and replace if necessary. 2). Inspect the laser shutter and make sure it is working properly. 3). Inspect the toner cartridge guide. 4). Clean the HV power supply contacts. 5). Replace transfer roller. 6). Replace engine controller board. 7). Replace laser/scanner cable assembly.

Model(s): All LX engine printers

Diagnosis: 1). Empty or defective toner cartridge. 2). Defective transfer roller. 3). Dirty or defective high voltage contacts. 4). Laser shutter not operating properly. 5). Defective high voltage power supply. 6). Defective DC controller.

Solution: 1). Inspect toner cartridge and replace if necessary. 2). Replace transfer roller. 3). Inspect high voltage contacts and clean or replace if necessary. 4). Inspect laser cover assembly and replace assembly if necessary. 5). Replace high voltage power supply. 6). Replace DC controller.

Model(s): All PX/VX engine printers

Diagnosis: 1). Empty or defective toner cartridge. 2). Defective transfer roller. 3). Dirty or defective high voltage connector springs. 4). Laser/scanner shutter door not operating properly. 5). Defective high voltage power supply. 6). Defective DC controller.

Solution: 1). Inspect toner cartridge and replace if necessary. 2). Replace transfer roller. 3). Inspect high voltage connector springs and clean or replace if necessary. 4). Inspect laser/scanner shutter door and replace laser/scanner assembly if necessary. 5). Replace high voltage power supply. 6). Replace DC controller.

Model(s): All AX engine printers and LaserJet 1100

Diagnosis: 1). Defective or empty toner cartridge. 2). Dirty HV contact points. 3). Poor laser/scanner connectors. 4). Defective laser/scanner. 5). Defective DC controller.

Solution: 1). Inspect toner cartridge and replace if necessary. 2). Clean HV contact points on toner cartridge and on transfer roller. 3). Inspect and reseat laser/scanner connectors. 4). Replace laser/scanner assembly. 5). Replace DC controller.

Model(s): All NX engine printers

Diagnosis: 1). Empty or defective toner cartridge. 2). Defective transfer roller. 3). Dirty or defective high voltage connector springs. 4). Laser/scanner shutter door not operating properly. 5). Defective high voltage power supply. 6). Defective DC controller.

Solution: 1). Inspect toner cartridge and replace if necessary. 2). Replace transfer roller. 3). Inspect high voltage connector springs and clean or replace if necessary. 4). Inspect laser/scanner shutter door and replace laser/scanner assembly if necessary. 5). Replace high voltage power supply.

Model(s): All WX engine printers

Diagnosis: 1). Empty or defective toner cartridge. 2). Defective transfer roller. 3). Dirty or defective high voltage connector springs. 4). Laser/scanner shutter door not operating properly. 5). Defective high voltage power supply. 6). Defective DC controller.

Solution: 1). Inspect toner cartridge and replace if necessary. 2). Replace transfer roller. 3). Inspect high voltage connector springs and clean or replace if necessary. 4). Inspect laser/scanner shutter door and replace laser/scanner assembly if necessary. 5. Replace high voltage power supply.

Model(s): All BX engine printers

Diagnosis: 1). Empty or defective toner cartridge. 2). Defective transfer roller. 3). Dirty or defective high voltage contacts. 4). Laser shutter not operating properly. 5). Defective high voltage power supply. 6). Defective DC controller.

Solution: 1). Inspect toner cartridge and replace if necessary. 2). Replace transfer roller. 3). Inspect high voltage contacts and clean or replace if necessary. 4). Inspect laser cover assembly and replace assembly if necessary. 5). Replace high voltage power supply. 6). Replace DC controller.

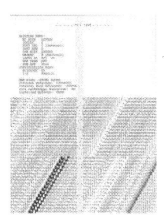

Problem: Faint smudge down page most visible when printing envelopes.

Model(s): All SX engine printers

Diagnosis: This is often caused by high static electricity in the air due to low humidity (mostly seen during the winter months).

Solution: Try adjusting the green toner density dial down. Also, try cleaning both the corona wire inside the toner cartridge and the transfer corona wire. If that fails, try swapping out the toner cartridge with a known good one. As a last resort. Replace the transfer corona.

Problem: Character voids.

Model(s): All SX engine printers

Diagnosis: 1). Print density improperly set. 2). Paper or media out of spec. 3). Defective fuser. 4). Defective HV power supply. 5). Defective DC controller.

Solution: 1). Try increasing density. 2). Try different paper or media. 3). Replace fuser assembly. 4). Replace HV power supply. 5). Replace DC controller.

Model(s): All EX engine printers

Diagnosis: 1). Laser shutter mechanism stuck or damaged. 2). Paper out of spec. 3). Dirty or defective transfer roller. 4). Defective fuser.

Solution: 1). Inspect laser shutter mechanism. 2). Try different paper. 3). Clean or replace transfer roller. 4). Inspect fuser assembly and replace if necessary.

Model(s): All NX engine printers

Diagnosis: 1). Paper out of spec. 2). Dirty or defective transfer roller. 3). Defective fuser.

Solution: 1). Try different paper. 2). Clean or replace transfer roller. 3). Inspect fuser assembly and replace if necessary.

Model(s): All WX engine printers

Diagnosis: 1). EconoMode enabled. 2). Paper out of spec. 3). Dirty or defective transfer roller. 4). Defective laser/scanner assembly.

Solution: 1). Disable EconoMode. 2). Try different paper. 3). Clean or replace transfer roller. 4). Replace laser/scanner assembly.

Problem: Wavy print.

Model(s): All SX engine printers

Diagnosis: 1). Defective laser/scanner cable. 2). Defective laser/scanner.

Solution: 1). Inspect laser/scanner cable and replace if necessary. 2). Replace laser/scanner assembly.

Model(s): IBM/Lexmark 4019/4029

Diagnosis: 1). Dirty or defective HVPS contact springs. 2). Poor transfer corona contacts. 3). Damaged gear train.

Solution: 1). Clean and inspect HVPS contacts. 2). Clean and inspect transfer corona contacts. 3). Inspect gear train and clean or replace if necessary.

Model(s): IBM/Lexmark 4039/4049

Diagnosis: 1). Dirty or defective HVPS contact springs. 2). Poor transfer roller contacts. 3). Damaged gear train.

Solution: 1). Clean and inspect HVPS contacts. 2). Clean and inspect transfer roller contacts. 3). Inspect gear train and clean or replace.

Problem: Horizontal fogged stripes.

Model(s): All SX engine printers

Diagnosis: 1). Defective toner cartridge. 2). Defective HV power supply cable. 3). Defective laser/scanner cable.

Solution: 1). Replace toner cartridge. 2). Inspect HV power supply cable and replace if necessary. 3). Inspect laser/scanner cable and replace if necessary.

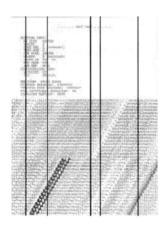

Problem: Vertical dark streaks.

Model(s): All SX engine printers

Diagnosis: 1). Dirty primary corona wire. 2). Defective toner cartridge. 3). Dirty cleaning wand. 4). Defective fuser.

Solution: 1). Clean primary corona wire. 2). Replace toner cartridge. 3). Inspect cleaning wand and replace if necessary. 4). Inspect fuser assembly and replace if necessary.

Model(s): IBM/Lexmark 4019/4029

Diagnosis: 1). Toner cartridge defective. 2). Print head shutter not functioning properly. 3). Dirty or defective HVPS contact springs. 4). Dirty or defective transfer corona.

Solution: 1). Inspect toner cartridge and replace if necessary. 2). Clean and inspect print head shutter. 3). Clean and inspect HVPS contacts. 4). Clean or replace transfer corona. 5). Inspect fuser assy. and replace if necessary.

Model(s): IBM/Lexmark 4039/4049

Diagnosis: 1). Toner cartridge defective. 2). Print head shutter not functioning properly. 3). Dirty or defective HVPS contact springs.

Solution: 1). Inspect toner cartridge and replace if necessary. 2). Clean and inspect print head shutter. 3). Clean and inspect HVPS contacts. 4). Inspect fuser assembly and replace if necessary.

Model(s): All EX engine printers

Diagnosis: Defective toner cartridge.

Solution: Replace toner cartridge.

Model(s): HP LaserJet 4000/4050

Diagnosis: 1). Defective toner cartridge. 2). Dirty or scratched fuser assembly.

Solution: 1). Inspect toner cartridge and replace if necessary. 2). Inspect fuser assembly and clean or replace if necessary.

Model(s): All PX/VX engine printers

Diagnosis: 1). Defective toner cartridge. 2). Static eliminator teeth dirty or defective. 3). Defective fuser.

Solution: 1). Inspect toner cartridge and replace if necessary. 2). Clean or replace static eliminator. 3). Inspect fuser assembly and replace if necessary.

Model(s): All AX engine printers and LaserJet 1100

Diagnosis: 1). Drum on toner cartridge damaged. 2). Paper path dirty. 3). Defective heating element or pressure roller.

Solution: 1). Inspect drum on toner cartridge and replace if necessary. 2). Clean paper path. 3). Inspect and replace if necessary, heating element and pressure roller.

Model(s): All NX engine printers

Diagnosis: 1). Defective toner cartridge. 2). Defective fuser.

Solution: 1). Replace toner cartridge. 2). Inspect fuser assembly and replace if necessary.

Model(s): All WX engine printers

Diagnosis: 1). Defective toner cartridge. 2). Static eliminator teeth dirty or defective. 3). Defective fuser.

Solution: 1). Inspect toner cartridge and replace if necessary. 2). Clean or replace static eliminator. 3). Inspect fuser assembly and replace if necessary.

Problem: Improperly sized image.

Model(s): All SX engine printers

Diagnosis: Defective paper tray micro switches.

Solution: Inspect paper tray micro switches.

Model(s): All EX engine printers

Diagnosis: 1). Defective paper tray switches. 2). MP Paper Size setting not set correctly.

Solution: 1). Inspect paper tray switches and replace if necessary. 2). Make sure MP Paper Size is set correctly.

Model(s): All NX engine printers

Diagnosis: Defective paper tray switches.

Solution: Inspect paper tray switches and replace if necessary.

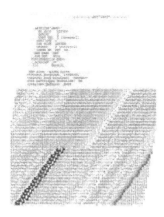

Problem: Image skew.

Model(s): All SX engine printers

Diagnosis: 1). Paper tray defective or loaded incorrectly. 2). Worn paper pickup roller.

Solution: 1). Inspect paper tray and verify that it is loaded correctly. 2). Inspect paper feed roller assembly and replace if necessary. 3). Replace registration assembly.

Model(s): IBM/Lexmark 4019/4029

Diagnosis: 1). Obstruction in paper path. 2). Defective paper tray. 3). Defective gear train.

Solution: 1). Inspect paper path for obstructions. 2). Inspect paper tray, replace if necessary. 3). Inspect gear train and clean or replace if necessary.

Model(s): IBM/Lexmark 4039/4049

Diagnosis: 1). Obstruction in paper path. 2). Defective paper tray. 3). Defective gear train.

Solution: 1). Inspect paper tray, replace if necessary. 2). Inspect gear train and clean or replace if necessary.

Model(s): All EX engine printers

Diagnosis: 1). Paper out of spec. 2). Defective input/registration sensor. 3). Worn or defective drive gears. 4). Defective paper tray.

Solution: 1). Try different paper. 2). Replace input/registration sensor. 3). Inspect and replace if necessary, drive gears and main drive assembly. 4). Inspect paper tray and replace if necessary.

Model(s): HP LaserJet 4000/4050

Diagnosis: 1). Paper trays not adjusted properly. 2). Registration assembly damaged or not installed correctly.

Solution: 1). Make sure paper guides are installed properly. 2). Inspect registration assembly and replace if necessary.

Model(s): All LX engine printers

Diagnosis: 1). Paper out of spec. 2). Worn paper pickup rollers and separation pad.

Solution: 1). Try different paper. 2). Inspect paper feed roller assembly and separation pad and replace if necessary.

Model(s): All PX/VX engine printers

Diagnosis: 1). Paper out of spec. 2). Worn pickup or registration rollers. 3). Beam-to-Drum mirror out of adjustment.

Solution: 1). Try different paper. 2). Inspect rollers and replace if necessary. 3). Adjust Beam-to-Drum mirror.

Model(s): All AX engine printers and LaserJet 1100

Diagnosis: 1). Paper guides out of adjustment. 2). Dirty or worn pickup roller and/or separation pad and sub pads.

Solution: 1). Readjust paper guides. 2). Clean or replace pickup roller and separation pads.

Model(s): All NX engine printers

Diagnosis: 1). Paper out of spec. 2). Defective registration assembly. 3). Worn or defective drive gears. 4). Defective paper tray.

Solution: 1). Try different paper. 2). Inspect and replace if necessary, registration assembly. 3). Inspect and replace if necessary, drive gears and main drive assembly. 4). Inspect paper tray and replace if necessary.

Model(s): All WX engine printers

Diagnosis: 1). Paper not loaded correctly. 2). Paper out of spec. 3). Worn pickup or registration rollers.

Solution: 1). Reload paper. 2). Try different paper. 3). Inspect and replace if necessary, pickup and registration rollers.

Problem: Portion of page blank.

Model(s): All SX engine printers

Diagnosis: Page is too complex, not enough memory.

Solution: Enable Page Protect and add additional memory.

Model(s): All LX engine printers

Diagnosis: Page is too complex, not enough memory.

Solution: Enable Page Protect and add additional memory.

Model(s): All PX/VX engine printers

Diagnosis: Page too complex.

Solution: Enable Page Protect and add additional memory.

Model(s): All AX engine printers and LaserJet 1100

Diagnosis: This usually indicates that the page being printed is too complex for the printer.

Solution: 1). Decrease resolution to 300 dpi through the printer software. 2). Install additional memory.

Model(s): All WX engine printers

Diagnosis: Page too complex.

Solution: Enable Page Protect and add additional memory.

Model(s): All BX engine printers

Diagnosis: Page is too complex, not enough memory.

Solution: Enable Page Protect and add additional memory.

Problem: Distorted or compressed print.

Model(s): All SX engine printers

Diagnosis: 1). Defective toner cartridge. 2). Problem with paper drive. 3). Defective laser/scanner cable. 4). Defective laser/scanner.

Solution: 1). Inspect toner cartridge and replace if necessary. 2). Inspect and replace if necessary, paper path drive mechanism, gear train and motor. 3). Inspect laser/scanner cable and replace if necessary.

Model(s): All EX engine printers

Diagnosis: 1). Binding in paper path. 2). Defective laser/scanner.

Solution: 1). Inspect and replace if necessary, toner cartridge, transport rollers, feed drive assembly, main motor and drive assembly and fuser assembly. 2). Replace laser/scanner assembly.

Model(s): HP LaserJet 4000/4050

Diagnosis: 1). Poor cable connections to laser/scanner. 2). Poor cable connections to engine controller board. 3). Defective laser/scanner.

Solution: 1). Inspect cables connected to laser/scanner. 2). Inspect cables connected to engine controller board. 3). Replace laser/scanner assembly.

Model(s): All AX engine printers

Diagnosis: 1). Excessive light getting into printer. 2). Dirty laser/scanner. 3). Poor laser/scanner connectors. 4). Defective laser/scanner. 5). Defective DC controller.

Solution: 1). Move printer out of the way of any direct light. 2). Blow out laser/scanner assembly. 3). Inspect and reseat laser/scanner connectors. 4). Replace laser/scanner assembly. 5). Replace DC controller.

Model(s): All NX engine printers

Diagnosis: 1). Binding in paper path. 2). Defective laser/scanner cable. 3). Defective laser/scanner.

Solution: 1). Inspect and replace if necessary, toner cartridge, transport rollers, feed drive assembly, main motor and drive assembly and fuser assembly. 2). Inspect laser/scanner cable and replace if necessary. 3). Replace laser/scanner assembly.

Model(s): All LX engine printers

Diagnosis: 1). Defective toner cartridge. 2). Defective drum drive gear.

Solution: 1). Inspect toner cartridge and replace if necessary. 2). Inspect drum drive gear assembly and replace if necessary.

Model(s): All PX/VX engine printers

Diagnosis: Defective toner cartridge.

Solution: Replace toner cartridge.

Model(s): All WX engine printers

Diagnosis: Defective toner cartridge.

Solution: Replace toner cartridge.

Problem: Black pages with white horizontal stipes.

Model(s): All SX engine printers

Diagnosis: 1). Defective fiber optic cable. 2). Defective laser/scanner. 3). Defective DC controller.

Solution: 1). Inspect fiber optic cable and replace if necessary. 2). Replace laser/scanner assembly. 3). Replace DC controller.

Model(s): All EX engine printers

Diagnosis: 1). Defective laser/scanner assembly. 2). Defective DC controller.

Solution: 1). Replace laser/scanner assembly. 2). Replace DC controller.

Model(s): All AX engine printers

Diagnosis: Defective toner cartridge.

Solution: Replace toner cartridge.

Model(s): All NX engine printers

Diagnosis: 1). Defective fiber-optic cable. 2). Defective laser/scanner. 3). Defective DC controller.

Solution: 1). Inspect fiber-optic cable and replace if necessary. 2). Replace laser/scanner assembly. 3). Replace DC controller.

Model(s): All WX engine printers

Diagnosis: 1). Defective toner cartridge. 2). Light leaking into printer. 3). Dirty or defective high voltage contact springs. 4). Poor connection between laser/scanner and DC controller. 5). Defective high voltage power supply. 6). Defective DC controller. 7). Defective laser/scanner.

Solution: 1). Inspect toner cartridge and replace if necessary. 2). Make sure all covers are closed. 3). Inspect high voltage connector springs and clean or replace if necessary. 4). Inspect connections between laser/scanner and DC controller. 5). Replace high voltage power supply. 6). Replace DC controller. 7). Replace laser/scanner assembly.

Problem: Repetitive Defects.

Model(s): All SX engine printers

Diagnosis: 1). Defective toner cartridge. 2). Defective fuser. 3). Defective HV power supply. 4). Defective DC controller.

Solution: 1). Inspect toner cartridge and replace if necessary. 2). Inspect fuser assembly and replace if necessary. 3). Replace HV power supply. 4). Replace DC controller.

Model(s): IBM/Lexmark 4019/4029

Diagnosis: 1). Defective toner cartridge. 2). Defective fuser. 3). Defective feed roller.

Solution: 1). Inspect toner cartridge and replace if necessary. 2). Inspect fuser assy. and replace if necessary. 3). Inspect feed roller and replace if necessary.

Model(s): IBM/Lexmark 4039/4049

Diagnosis: 1). Defective toner cartridge. 2). Defective transfer roller. 3). Defective fuser. 4). Defective feed roller.

Solution: 1). Inspect toner cartridge and replace if necessary. 2). Inspect transfer roller and replace if necessary. 3). Inspect fuser assembly and replace if necessary. 4). Inspect feed roller and replace if necessary.

Model(s): All EX engine printers

Diagnosis: 1). Defective toner cartridge. 2). Defective transfer roller. 3). Defective fuser assembly.

Solution: 1). Inspect and replace if necessary, toner cartridge. 2). Inspect and replace if necessary, transfer roller. 3). Inspect and replace if necessary, fuser assembly.

Model(s): HP LaserJet 4000/4050

Diagnosis: 1). Printer needs cleaning. 2). Damaged drum on toner cartridge. 3). Damaged transfer roller. 4). Damaged fuser.

Solution: 1). Clean printer. 2). Inspect toner cartridge and replace if necessary. 3). Inspect transfer roller and replace if necessary. 4). Inspect fuser assembly and replace if necessary.

Model(s): All LX engine printers

Diagnosis: 1). Defective toner cartridge. 2). Drive gears are worn. 3). Fiber optic cable defective. 4). Defective laser/scanner. 5). Defective DC controller.

Solution: 1). Inspect toner cartridge and replace if necessary. 2). Inspect drive gears and replace if necessary. 3). Inspect fiber optic cable and replace if necessary. 4). Replace laser/scanner assembly. 5). Replace DC controller.

Model(s): All PX/VX engine printers

Diagnosis: 1). Defective toner cartridge. 2). Dirty paper path. 3). Defective transfer roller. 4). Defective fuser assembly. 5). Worn drive gear.

Solution: 1). Inspect and replace if necessary, toner cartridge. 2). Inspect paper path and clean if necessary. 3). Inspect transfer roller and replace if necessary. 4). Inspect and replace if necessary, fuser assembly. 5). Inspect gear train assembly and replace if necessary.

Model(s): All AX engine printers

Diagnosis: 1). Printer needs cleaning. 2). Damaged drum on toner cartridge. 3). Damaged transfer roller. 4). Damaged heating element or pressure roller.

Solution: 1). Clean printer. 2). Inspect toner cartridge and replace if necessary. 3). Inspect transfer roller and replace if necessary. 4). Inspect pressure roller and heating element and replace if necessary.

Model(s): All NX engine printers

Diagnosis: 1). Defective toner cartridge. 2). Defective transfer roller. 3). Defective fuser assembly. 4). Defective HV power supply.

Solution: 1). Inspect and replace if necessary, toner cartridge. 2). Inspect and replace if necessary, transfer roller. 3). Inspect and replace if necessary, fuser assembly. 4). Replace high voltage power supply.

Model(s): All WX engine printers

Diagnosis: 1). Defective toner cartridge. 2). Dirty or defective transfer roller. 3). Dirty or defective fuser.

Solution: 1). Inspect toner cartridge and replace if necessary. 2). Clean or replace transfer roller. 3). Clean or replace fuser assembly.

Problem: Black stripe on right or left side of page.

Model(s): All SX engine printers

Diagnosis: Dirty primary corona wire.

Solution: Clean primary corona wire.

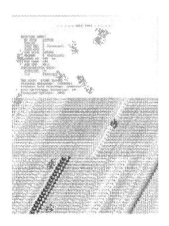

Problem: Background scatter.

Model(s): All SX engine printers

Diagnosis: 1). Print density improperly set. 2). Paper out of spec. 3). Dirty primary corona wire. 4). Defective toner cartridge. 5). Dirty or defective transfer corona wire. 6). Inside of printer dirty.

Solution: 1). Adjust print density. 2). Try different paper. 3). Clean primary corona wire. 4). Replace toner cartridge. 5). Clean or replace transfer corona wire. 6). Clean inside of printer.

Model(s): IBM/Lexmark 4019/4029

Diagnosis: 1). Dirty or defective toner cartridge. 2). Defective or defective transfer corona. 3). Dirty or defective HVPS contact springs.

Solution: 1). Clean erase lamps on toner cartridge or replace cartridge if necessary. 2). Clean or replace transfer corona. 3). Inspect HVPS contact springs.

Model(s): IBM/Lexmark 4039/4049

Diagnosis: 1). Dirty or defective toner cartridge. 2). Defective transfer roller. 3). Dirty or defective HVPS contact springs.

Solution: 1). Clean erase lamps on toner cartridge or replace cartridge if necessary. 2). Replace transfer roller. 3). Inspect HVPS contact springs and clean or replace if necessary.

Model(s): All EX engine printers

Diagnosis: 1). Paper out of spec. 2). Print density setting set too low. 3). Paper path dirty. 4). Defective toner cartridge.

Solution: 1). Try different paper. 2). Adjust print density setting. 3). Clean paper path. 4). Replace toner cartridge.

Model(s): All LX engine printers

Diagnosis: 1). Print density improperly set. 2). Paper out of spec. 4). Defective toner cartridge. 5). Dirty or defective transfer roller. 6). Inside of printer dirty.

Solution: 1). Adjust print density. 2). Try different paper. 3). Replace toner cartridge. 4). Clean or replace transfer roller. 5). Clean inside of printer.

Model(s): All PX/VX engine printers

Diagnosis: 1). Paper out of spec. 2). Print density setting set too low. 3). Paper path dirty. 4). Dirty or defective transfer rollers. 5). Defective toner cartridge.

Solution: 1). Try different paper. 2). Adjust print density setting. 3). Clean paper path. 4). Clean or replace transfer roller. 5). Replace toner cartridge.

Model(s): All NX engine printers

Diagnosis: 1). Paper out of spec. 2). Print density setting set too low. 3). Paper path dirty. 4). Defective toner cartridge.

Solution: 1). Try different paper. 2). Adjust print density setting. 3). Clean paper path. 4). Replace toner cartridge.

Model(s): All WX engine printers

Diagnosis: 1). Paper out of spec. 2). Print density setting set too low. 3). Dirty paper path. 4). Defective toner cartridge. 5). Dirty or defective transfer roller. 6). Toner buildup in fuser inlet guide.

Solution: 1). Try different paper. 2). Set density to darker setting. 3). Clean paper path. 4). Inspect toner cartridge and replace if necessary. 5). Clean or replace transfer roller. 6). Clean fuser inlet guide.

Model(s): All BX engine printers

Diagnosis: 1). Print density improperly set. 2). Paper out of spec. 4). Defective toner cartridge. 5). Dirty or defective transfer roller. 6). Inside of printer dirty.

Solution: 1). Adjust print density. 2). Try different paper. 3). Replace toner cartridge. 4). Clean or replace transfer roller. 5). Clean inside of printer.

Problem: Residual Image.

Model(s): All SX engine printers

Diagnosis: 1). Defective toner cartridge. 2). Defective fuser.

Solution: 1). Replace toner cartridge. 2). Inspect fuser assembly and replace if necessary.

Model(s): All EX engine printers

Diagnosis: 1). Defective toner cartridge. 2). Defective fuser.

Solution: 1). Replace toner cartridge. 2). Inspect fuser assembly and replace if necessary.

Model(s): All LX/PX/VX engine printers

Diagnosis: 1). Defective toner cartridge. 2). Defective fuser.

Solution: 1). Replace toner cartridge. 2). Inspect fuser assembly and replace if necessary.

Model(s): All WX engine printers

Diagnosis: 1). Defective toner cartridge. 2). Defective fuser.

Solution: 1). Replace toner cartridge. 2). Inspect fuser assembly and replace if necessary.

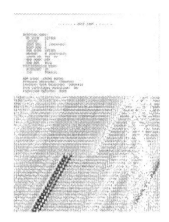

Problem: Missing text on right side.

Model(s): All EX engine printers

Diagnosis: 1). Low toner. 2). Laser shutter mechanism stuck or damaged.

Solution: 1). Shake toner cartridge to redistribute toner or replace cartridge. 2). Inspect laser shutter mechanism.

Model(s): All NX engine printers

Diagnosis: 1). Low toner. 2). Beam-to-drum mirror out of alignment.

Solution: 1). Shake toner cartridge to redistribute toner or replace cartridge. 2). Inspect beam-to-drum mirror.

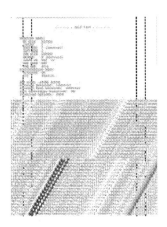

Problem: Vertical dots.

Model(s): HP LaserJet 4000/4050

Diagnosis: 1). Dirty static eliminator. 2). Defective transfer roller. 3). Defective engine controller.

Solution: 1). Clean static eliminator and contacts to engine controller board. 2). Replace transfer roller. 3). Replace engine controller board.

Problem: Horizontal white lines.

Model(s): HP LaserJet 4000/4050

Diagnosis: 1). Defective toner cartridge. 2). Defective fuser. 3). Defective laser/scanner. 4). Defective engine controller.

Solution: 1). Inspect toner cartridge and replace if necessary. 2). Inspect fuser assembly and replace if necessary. 3). Replace laser/scanner assembly. 4). Replace engine controller board.

Model(s): All WX engine printers

Diagnosis: 1). Low toner. 2). Defective toner cartridge. 3). Object blocking beam path.

Solution: 1). Shake toner cartridge to redistribute toner or replace cartridge. 2). Replace toner cartridge. 3). Inspect path between toner cartridge and laser/scanner assembly.

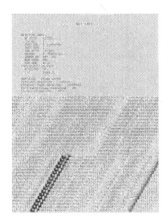

Problem: Dark background.

Model(s): HP LaserJet 4000/4050

Diagnosis: 1). Toner density setting needs adjustment. 2). Defective toner cartridge.

Solution: 1). Adjust toner density setting through software. 2). Replace toner cartridge.

Model(s): All AX engine printers

Diagnosis: 1). Toner density setting needs adjustment. 2). Dirty HV contact points. 3). Defective laser/scanner. 4). Defective DC controller.

Solution: 1). Adjust toner density setting through software. 2). Clean HV contact points on toner cartridge and on transfer roller. 3). Replace laser/scanner assembly. 4). Replace DC controller.

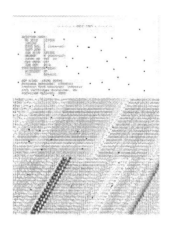

Problem: Toner specks.

Model(s): HP LaserJet 4000/4050

Diagnosis: Dirty paper path.

Solution: Clean printer (print cleaning page).

Problem: Bubble print.

Model(s): All PX/VX engine printers

Diagnosis: 1). Paper out of spec. 2). Dirty paper path. 3). Dirty or defective transfer roller. 4). Dirty fuser assembly. 5). Defective toner cartridge.

Solution: 1). Try different paper. 2). Clean paper path. 3). Clean or replace transfer roller. 4). Clean fuser assembly. 5). Inspect toner cartridge and replace if necessary.

Model(s): All NX engine printers

Diagnosis: 1). Defective toner cartridge. 2). Dirty drum ground contacts on high voltage power supply. 3). Defective high voltage power supply.

Solution: 1). Inspect toner cartridge and replace if necessary. 2). Clean and inspect high voltage power supply connectors. 3). Replace high voltage power supply.

Model(s): All WX engine printers

Diagnosis: 1). Toner cartridge not grounded properly. 2). Paper out of spec. 3). Defective toner cartridge. 4). Defective high voltage power supply.

Solution: 1). Make sure toner cartridge is seated properly. 2). Try different paper. 3). Replace toner cartridge. 4). Replace high voltage power supply.

Problem: Line at top edge of paper.

Model(s): All WX engine printers

Diagnosis: Defective toner cartridge.

Solution: Replace toner cartridge.

Problem: Blank line in the middle of the page (Tray 4 input only).

Model(s): All WX engine printers

Diagnosis: 1). Defective clutch in vertical transfer door. 2). Defective clutch in paper pickup assembly.

Solution: 1). Replace Tray 4 vertical transfer door. 2). Replace Tray 4 paper pickup assembly.

APPENDIX A—ERROR CODES AND MESSAGES

Hewlett-Packard

02 Warming Up (>3 Minutes) Also See 50 Error

II, IID

- Defective or incorrectly installed I/O cable.
- Defective formatter PCA.

IIISi/4Si

- Defective display cable.
- Defective formatter PCA.

4V

- Defective or incorrectly installed I/O cable.
- Defective fusing assembly, DC controller, PCA power supply or formatter PCA.

11 Paper Out (MP/PC/UC/LC/EC/LE LOAD)

All Printers

- Paper tray empty or not seated correctly.
- Paper sensor arm stuck or is broken.
- Incorrect or defective tray size sensing—Inspect and verify tray tabs and switches and/or control panel settings.
- Defective paper control/sensor PCA.

4L

- Missing or empty paper cassette.
- Paper cassette not seated correctly.
- Paper out flag PS2 stuck or broken.
- Defective DC controller.

12 Printer Open

All Printers (Except IIP, IIP Plus, IIIP and 4P)

- Printer door open.
- Defective DC power supply.
- Defective DC controller.
- Missing top cover tab.

4V

- Stuck or broken front door open sensor flag.
- Stuck or broken toner cartridge micro switch.
- Defective DC controller PCA.

4, 4 Plus

- Top cover plunger missing.
- Defective paper control PCA.

IIISi, 4Si

- Stuck or broken PS1.
- Burnt out fuser bulb.
- Defective DC controller PCA.

12 Open or No EP

IIP, IIP Plus, IIIP

- Open paper path door.
- No toner cartridge or toner cartridge defective or not seated correctly.
- Defective fan, PS4 or PS5.

4L

- Top cover open.
- Top cover plunger broken.

4P

- Top cover open.
- Toner cartridge not installed.
- Defective interlock switch assembly.

13 Paper Jam/Remove Paper Jam

All Printers

- Media does not meet printer specifications.
- Paper path blocked.
- Worn paper pickup roller(s) and/or separation pad(s).
- Incorrect paper length or size setting.
- Stuck or broken paper exit sensor flag.
- Stuck or broken paper input sensor.
- Paper not loaded correctly.
- Defective solenoid.
- Damaged drive train gear(s).
- Defective main motor.
- Defective main motor drive circuitry.
- Defective DC controller.

II, III

- Defective or obstructed registration assembly.
- Defective or obstructed fusing assembly.
- Defective sensor cable from fuser to DC controller.

IID, IIID

- Defective or obstructed registration assembly.
- Defective or obstructed fusing assembly.
- Defective or obstructed paper duplexer.
- Misadjusted switchback assembly.

4, 4 Plus

- Rear door open.
- Broken or missing cassette paper-out sensor flag.
- 500-sheet lower cassette adjusted incorrectly.
- Transfer roller not seated correctly.
- Defective input sensor (PS1).
- Defective fuser exit sensor (PS3).

- Defective paper-end sensor (PS5) if it jams from the MP tray (Tray 1).
- Defective output rollers.

4L, 4P

- Rear door open.
- Stuck or broken paper flags.
- Obstruction under oblique rollers.
- Transfer roller not seated correctly.

4V

- Defective toner cartridge.
- Worn paper path gears.
- Defective DC controller PCA.
- Defective or obstructed registration guide.

5P, 6P

- Obstruction under oblique rollers.
- Stuck or broken paper flags.
- Defective DC controller.

5L, 6L

- Worn separation pad and/or secondary pads.
- Stuck or broken paper flags.
- Defective DC controller.

13.xx Paper Jam

IIISi, 4Si

1= Internal—Check entire paper path for obstruction.

2= Input—Check paper input path and paper re-feed from duplex unit.

3= Duplex—Check PS4 or PS5 in duplex or switchback.

4= Output—Check PS7 in output area Optional Power Stacker.

5Si

0 = Non-specific jam.

1 = Paper feed/paper late jam—Inspect flag PS2 located in paper pickup.

2 = Paper feed/paper late jam—Inspect registration photo sensor.

3 = Fuser output paper late jam—Inspect PS 1403 located in fuser.

4 = Fuser output paper jam.

5, 6 = Duplex module paper jam—Inspect diverter drive assembly and PS402 located in face-down delivery assembly.

7-10 = Duplex module paper jam—Inspect duplex assembly.

11 = External input device jam—Inspect 2000-Sheet Input Tray.

12 = External output device paper jam—Inspect Multibin Mailbox/Stapler.

13 = Fuser accordion jam—Inspect fuser assembly.

14 = Printer could not auto-eject the paper—Inspect entire paper path.

4000

1, 2 = Paper delay or stop jam at feed area—Inspect paper trays, input and registration areas for obstructions. Inspect PS102 and PS103.

5, 6 = Paper delay or stop jam at fuser—Inspect paper path before fuser for obstructions. Inspect PS501 and PS106.

10 = Paper jam at duplexer—Inspect duplexer for obstructions. Replace duplexer if necessary.

20 = Paper stop jam in paper path—Inspect entire paper path for obstructions.

21 = Door open jam—Ensure that all doors are closed.

14 No EP Cartridge or Toner Cartridge

All Printers
- Toner cartridge not installed or seated properly.
- Defective toner cartridge.

II, IID, III, IIID
- Defective paper control PCA.

4, 4 Plus
- HVPS contacts dirty or misaligned.
- Defective HVPS.

4V

- Toner cartridge micro switch on high voltage PCA bent or broken.
- Front-door-open sensor flag PS402 stuck or defective.
- Defective DC controller PCA.

IIISi, 4Si

- Broken or bent tabs on toner cartridge.
- Switch actuator support tab on DC controller bent or broken.
- Defective HVPS.

16 Toner Low

All Printers

- Defective toner cartridge.
- Defective HVPS.

II, III

- DC controller to HVPS cable defective.

IIISi, 4Si

- Door-open sensor flag PS1 defective.
- Toner level sensor defective.
- Defective DC controller PCA.

18 MIO Not Ready

- Printer not connected to active network port.
- Defective or misaligned MIO card.

18 MIO Initialization

- Printer not connected to active network port.
- Defective or misaligned MIO card.

20 Error/Memory Overflow/Insufficient Memory

All Printers

- Print job exceeds memory capacity—Add memory or simplify print job.

5

- Too much data or data too complex—Enable Image Adapt and Page Protect.

5L, 6L

- Set enhanced I/O to auto mode.

21 Error/Print Overrun/Page Too Complex

All Printers

- Print job too complex—Add memory or simplify print job.

IIIP, III, IIID

- With 1MB extra memory installed, Enable Page Protect.

4, 4M, 4 Plus, 4M Plus

- Enable Page Protect.

4L, 5L, 6L, 5P, 6P, 5, 5Si, 4000

- Enable Page Protect.

22 Error/I/O Config Error/Par I/O/Serial I/O/MIO/EIO Error

All Printers

- Check I/O configuration settings.
- Defective or incorrect printer cable.
- Computer powered off.
- Defective MIO/EIO or formatter PCA.

23 I/O Not Ready

- I/O card defective or not seated correctly.

24 Job Memory Full

- Print job too complex—Add memory or simplify print job.

25 XXX Memory Full

- Print job too complex—Add memory or simplify print job.

30 PS Error 16

- Check I/O connections and media requests.

30 PS Error 22 or 25

- Defective PostScript SIMM.

30 PS Error XX (other)

- PCL file sent to printer while in PostScript mode.

30.1.1 Disk Failure

5Si

- Optional disk has failed.

40 Error/Bad Serial Transmission

- Computer and printer set to different baud rates.
- Computer powered off.
- MIO card defective or not seated correctly.
- Abnormal connection break between computer and printer.

40.x MIO Error/EIO x Bad Transmission

5Si, 4000

1 = Connection break in slot 1 MIO/EIO—Reseat or replace if problem persists.

2 = Connection break in slot 2 MIO/EIO—Reseat or replace if problem persists.

41 Error (Temporary Print Engine Failure)

All Printers

- Temporary error has occurred—Reset printer.

II, IID, III, IIID

- Defective fiber optic cable.
- Defective laser scanner cable.
- Defective laser scanner assembly.

IIP

- Replace fuser with updated fuser assembly.

IIP, IIP Plus, IIIP

- Defective fiber optic cable.
- Paper feed problem.

5L, 6L

- Reseat formatter PCA.
- Replace formatter PCA.
- Replace DC controller PCA.

41.1, 41.2 or 41.3 Error (Unexpected Paper Size)

All Printers

- Bad laser scanner connections.
- Incorrect size paper being used.
- Paper size setting does not match installed paper.
- Paper cassette overfilled or not adjusted properly.
- Media does not meet printer specifications.

5, 5Si

1 = Defective connections—Check laser scanner connections.

2 = Beam detect malfunction—Check laser scanner connections.

3 = Paper size selection does not match installed paper.

4000

- Paper size selection does not match installed paper.

41.4 or 41.5 Error

All Printers

- Defective DC controller.
- Defective formatter PCA.

IIISi, 4Si

- Defective toner cartridge.

5, 5Si

> 4 = Sync error—Reseat DC controller and formatter PCA connections.
>
> 5 = Video sync or undetermined error—Reseat DC controller and formatter.

41.x Printer Error

- Inspect connections between laser scanner and engine control board.
- Replace laser scanner.
- Replace engine control board.

50 Error/50 Service (Fuser Error)

All Printers

- Temporary error occurred—Turn printer off for 20 minutes to clear error.
- Low or unstable power to printer.

II, IID, III, IIID

- Defective fuser.
- Defective AC power module.
- Defective DC power supply.

IIP, IIP Plus, IIIP

- Defective fuser.
- Defective power supply.

IIISi, 4Si

- Fuser not seated correctly.
- Sensor PCA connector J201 not connected properly.
- Switch SW101 not engaged.

4L, 4P, 4V

- Fuser not seated correctly.
- Defective fuser.

4, 4 Plus, 5

- Defective fuser.
- Defective power supply.

5P, 6P

- Defective fuser.
- Defective DC controller.

5L, 6L

- Defective heating element.
- Defective DC controller.

50.x Fuser Error

5Si, 4000

1 = Fuser low temperature failure

2 = Warm up failure.

3 = Over temperature failure.

4 = Defective fuser.

5 = Inconsistent fuser temperature (4000).

51 Error (Loss of Beam Detect)

II, IID, III, IIID

- Toner cartridge not seated properly.
- Laser shutter not operating properly.
- Defective fiber optic cable.
- Defective laser scanner assembly.

IIP, IIP Plus, IIIP

- Toner cartridge not seated properly.
- Laser shutter not operating properly.
- Defective fiber optic cable.
- Defective laser PCA.

IIISi, 4Si

- Toner cartridge not seated properly.
- Defective fiber optic cable.
- Reseat connections J002 on DC controller and J601 on laser PCA.
- Defective laser scanner assembly.

4V

- Defective fiber optic cable.
- Defective laser scanner assembly.

4, 4 Plus, 5

- Bad connections to laser scanner.
- Defective laser scanner assembly.

4L, 4P, 5L, 5P, 6L, 6P

- Temporary error—Cycle power to printer.
- Laser scanner assembly not seated correctly.
- Defective laser scanner assembly.

51.x Error (Printer Error)

5Si, 4000

1= Beam detect malfunction—Inspect laser scanner and cables, replace if necessary.

2= Laser malfunction—Inspect laser scanner and cables, replace if necessary.

52 Error (Incorrect Scanner Speed)

II, IID, III, IIID

- Defective laser scanner cable to DC controller.
- Defective laser scanner assembly.

IIP, IIP Plus, IIIP

- Defective scanner motor.
- Defective DC controller.

4, 4 Plus, 5

- Defective laser scanner cable.
- Defective laser scanner assembly.

4L, 4P, 5L, 5P, 6L, 6P

- Temporary error—Cycle power to the printer.
- Scanner assembly not seated correctly.

- Defective laser scanner cable.
- Defective laser scanner assembly.
- Defective DC controller PCA.

IIISi, 4Si, 4V

- Defective cable to DC controller.
- Defective laser scanner assembly
- Defective DC controller.

52.x Error (Printer Error)

5Si, 4000

1= Scanner startup failure—Reseat cables. Replace laser scanner assembly.

2= Scanner rotation failure—Reseat cables. Replace laser scanner assembly.

53 Error (Accessory Memory Error)

II, IID

- Memory card failure.

III, IIID

- 53.1 Error—Front memory card failure.
- 53.2 Error—Rear memory card failure.

IIP, IIP Plus, IIIP

- 53 Error Unit 1—Top memory card failure.
- 53 Error Unit 2—Bottom memory card failure.

IIISi, 4Si

- Temporary memory—Cycle power to printer.
- Laser malfunction—See 51 Error.

53.xy.zz Error

4, 4P, 4 Plus, 4V, 4Si, 5, 5P, 5Si, 6P, 4000

X (Hardware Type)	ZZ (Error Number)
0 = ROM Error 1 = RAM Error 2 = Flash Error	0 = Unsupported memory 1 = Unrecognized memory 2 = Unsupported memory size 3 = Failed RAM test
Y (Hardware Device)	4 = Exceeded maximum RAM size
0 = Internal memory (Formatter PCA) 1 = SIMM/DIMM Slot 1 2 = SIMM/DIMM Slot 2 3 = SIMM/DIMM Slot 3 4 = SIMM/DIMM Slot 4	5 = Exceeded maximum ROM size 6 = Invalid SIMM/DIMM speed 7 = SIMM/DIMM reporting information incorrectly 8 = SIMM/DIMM RAM parity error 9 = ROM mapped to unsupported address 10 = SIMM/DIMM address conflict 11 = ROM out of bounds 12 = Could not make temporary mapping

- Cycle power to printer.
- Reseat or replace SIMM/DIMM.

4L, 5L, 6L

- Temporary error—Cycle power to printer.
- Defective memory card.
- Defective formatter PCA.

54 Error

IID, IID

- Duplex feed error—Inspect duplex shift plate and PS5 or SL4.
- Replace duplex unit.

5Si

- Duplexer defective—Replace duplexer.

55 Error (Internal Communication Problem)

All Printers

- Defective DC controller PCA.
- Defective formatter PCA.

- Defective paper input PCA.
- Defective main motor.
- Inadequate power to printer.

4V

- Defective laser scanner assembly.

IIISi, 4Si

- Inspect connectors on LVPS and DC controller PCA.
- Inspect cable between DC controller and formatter PCA.
- Defective DC power supply.

4000

- Check for adequate AC power to printer.
- Replace formatter PCA.
- Replace engine control board.

56 Error

IID, IIID

- Output selector knob not in duplex position.

IIISi, 4Si

- Trying to print envelope in duplex mode.

56.x Error

5Si, 4000

1 = Invalid input source—Check or reselect input device.
2 = Invalid output destination—Check or reselect output device.

57 Error

III, IIID

- 57-1 Error—Incompatible memory card in front slot.
- 57-2 Error—Incompatible memory card in rear slot.

IIP, IIP Plus, IIIP

- 57 Error Unit 1—Incompatible memory card in top slot.
- 57 Error Unit 2—Incompatible memory card in bottom slot.

4L, 4, 5, 5P, 6P

- Defective main motor.

5L, 6L

- Incompatible memory card.

57.x Service

IIISi, 4Si

1 = Check J010 on DC controller PCA, main motor, main motor PCA.

2 = Fan 1 defective.

3 = Fan 2 defective.

4 = Fan 3 defective.

4 Plus

- Gears have seized.
- Main motor defective
- DC controller PCA defective.

5

- Main motor defective.

5Si

2 = Fan 1 defective.

3 = Fan 2 defective.

4 = Fan 3 defective.

4000

4 = Printer fan failure.

7 = Duplexer fan failure.

58 Service

4V

- Defective DC controller PCA.

4, 4L, 4P, 4V, 5, 5P, 6P

- Inspect fan cable.
- Fan is defective.

58.1 or 58.2 Error

- Paper cassette not installed properly.

58.x Printer Error

5Si

1 = Tray 2 lifter malfunction—Replace tray 2 lifter.

2 = Tray 3 lifter malfunction—Replace tray 3 lifter.

3 = Tray 1 lifter malfunction—Replace tray 1 lifter.

4 = Tray 4 lifter malfunction—Replace tray 4 lifter.

59 Add Memory

- Not enough memory installed to support PostScript option—Install additional memory.

59.x Printer Error

5Si, 4000

1 = Main motor startup failure—Inspect main motor and replace if necessary.

2 = Main motor rotation failure—Inspect main motor and replace if necessary.

60 Service

4, 4 Plus, 4P

- Defective formatter PCA.

60-62 Memory

IIISi, 4Si, 4V

- Defective SIMM(s).

61 Service or 62 Service

II, IID, IIP, IIP Plus, III, IIID, IIIP, 4P

- Defective formatter PCA.

61.x Service

- SIMM in slot x defective.
- Defective formatter PCA.

62.x Service/Printer Error, 62.0 Service, 62.1-4 Service, 62.5 Service or 62.6 Service

All Printers

- Font cartridge or SIMM(s) not installed correctly.
- Defective internal memory—replace formatter PCA.
- SIMM in slot x defective.
- Font cartridge (x=5) defective.

4V

- Defective cache.

4000

0 = Internal memory error.

1-4 = DIMM slot x error—Reseat or replace DIMM.

63 Service

II, IID, IIP Plus, III, IIID, IIIP, 4, 4 Plus, 4V, 4P, 5, 5L, 5P, 6L, 6P

- Defective formatter PCA.

IIISi, 4Si, 4V

- Defective SIMM(s).

64 Service/Printer Error

All Printers

- Power cycle printer.
- Defective formatter PCA.

5Si

- Power cycle printer.
- Defective controller PCA.

65 Memory

IIISi, 4Si, 4V

- Defective SIMM(s).

65 Service

All Printers (except IIISi, 4Si)

- Defective formatter PCA.

IIISi, 4Si, 4V

- Temporary error—Cycle power to printer.

65 Printer Error

5, 5P, 6P, 5Si

- Dynamic RAM error—Replace formatter PCA.

66.x.yy Device Error

5Si

X (Paper-Handling Device)	YY (Paper-Handling Device Error Code)
0 = EPH PCA 1 = First device attached to EPH 2 = Second device attached to EPH 3 = Third device attached to EPH 4 = Fourth device attached to EPH 5 = Fifth device attached to EPH	01-22, 24 = Check cabling and mechanical interface between printer and device. Replace external paper-handling PCA. 23 = Check cabling and mechanical interface between printer and device. Replace external paper-handling PCA. Replace defective device. 31 = Printer not supported by paper-handling device 1. 32 = Printer not supported by paper-handling device 2. 33 = Printer not supported by paper-handling device 3. 34 = Printer not supported by paper-handling device 4. 35 = Printer not supported by paper-handling device 5. 41 = Device 1 reports invalid configuration. 42 = Device 2 reports invalid configuration. 43 = Device 3 reports invalid configuration. 44 = Device 4 reports invalid configuration. 45 = Device 5 reports invalid configuration.

4000

1st x—Device number in chain.

2nd x—Device type (1—Input, 2—Output, 3—Stapler/stacker).

yy—Device error code.

67 Service/Printer Error

II, IID, IIP, IIP Plus, III, IIID, IIIP, 4, 4 Plus, 4P, 5

- Defective formatter PCA.

4Si, 4V

- Temporary error—Cycle power to printer.
- Defective paper guide and plate assembly.

5Si

- Field replacement units (FRUs) not installed correctly.

67, 68 Memory

IIISi, 4Si, 4V

- Defective SIMM(s).

68 Error/Service

All Printers

- Temporary error—Cycle power to printer.
- Defective formatter PCA.

4, 4 Plus, 4P, 5, 5P, 5Si, 6P, 4000

68 SERVICE—NVRAM FULL—Perform NVRAM initialization.
68 ERROR—NVRAM ERROR—Perform NVRAM initialization.

69 Service

- Defective I/O PCA.
- Defective formatter PCA.

69.x Printer Error

- Power cycle printer
- Reseat duplexer.

70-71 Error

All Printers

- Incompatible cartridge or SIMM installed in font or SIMM slot.

5Si

- Defective MIO card.

72 Service

- Defective font cartridge.
- Defective formatter PCA.

79 Service/Printer Error

All Printers

- Check software/drivers, memory PCAs, font cartridges and optional I/O cards.
- Defective formatter PCA.

5Si, 4000

1—Cycle power to printer.

2—Check interface cable.

3—Check SIMM/DIMM(s).

4—Check MIO/EIO card(s).

5—Try using parallel interface.

6—Remove MIO/EIO cards, perform cold reset.

7—Replace formatter PCA.

80 MIO Failure

- Check pins on MIO.
- Defective MIO card.
- Defective formatter PCA.

81 Error

- Defective formatter PCA.

89 PostScript ROM Failure

- Inspect PostScript ROM for bent pins.
- Verify that PostScript ROMs/SIMM installed correctly.
- Cycle power to printer.
- Defective ROMs/SIMM.

8x.yyyy

4000

1,6 = Error with EIO in slot 1—Reseat or replace if problem persists.

2,7 = Error with EIO in slot 2—Reseat or replace if problem persists.

Display is All Block Characters

- Inspect LCD display cable.
- Defective control panel.
- Defective formatter PCA.

Blank Display (LCD)

All Printers

- Check for AC and DC voltages.
- Inspect display panel and cabling.
- Defective formatter PCA or DC controller.

4V

- Check CB101 and F101.
- Defective control panel or formatter PCA.

Blank Display (All LEDs Off)

4L

- Printer is in sleep mode.
- Check for power to printer.
- Inspect fuses FU101 and FU201 on DC controller PCA.
- Inspect cable between DC controller and formatter PCA.
- Defective DC controller or formatter PCA.

5L, 6L

- Printer is in sleep mode.
- Check for power to printer.
- Inspect control panel PCA cable.
- Inspect fuses on DC controller.
- Defective DC controller or formatter PCA.

ALL LEDs On

4L, 5L, 6L

- Power cycle printer.

- Service error—Hold down button to display error code.
- Defective formatter PCA.

Data and Ready LEDs Blinking

5L, 6L

- Firmware error.

Data LED Blinking

5L, 6L

- Printer set to manual feed.
- Inspect paper input sensor (PS1).

Error LED Always On

5L, 6L

- Power cycle printer.
- Inspect connector between formatter and DC controller PCA.
- Defective formatter or DC controller PCA.

Tray 1 LED Blinking

6P

- Printer set to manual feed.

FS Disk Failure

4V

- Temporary error—Power cycle printer.
- Inspect disk drive and replace if necessary.

IBM/Lexmark

22 Paper Jam

- Incorrect paper size.
- Defective (pickup) D-Roller.
- Item in paper path.
- Defective paper path drive gear(s).
- Defective paper tray.
- Defective input sensor flag or sensor board.
- Defective system cable 2 or system board.

23 Paper Jam

- Incorrect paper size.
- Defective (pickup) D-Roller.
- Item in paper path.
- Defective paper path drive gear(s).
- Defective paper tray.
- Defective exit sensor flag or exit sensor board (check fuser).
- Defective system cable 1 or system board.

24 Invalid Manual Feed

- Paper fed into Manual Feed while printing from paper tray.

30 Open Cover

- Toner cartridge not installed or installed incorrectly.
- Top cover switch activator bent or broken.
- Defective low voltage power supply.
- Defective high voltage power supply.
- Defective system cable 2 or system board.

31 Change Paper

- Incorrect size paper installed.
- Check software paper size settings.
- Defective system board.

31 Change Envelope

- Incorrect size envelope installed.
- Check software envelope size settings.
- Defective system board.

35 Paper Error

- See 23 Paper Jam

36 Load Paper

- See 23 Paper Jam

37 Stop Command Received

- Press Start/Stop to clear error.
- Check software setup.
- Defective system board.

40 System Board Failure

- Defective system board.

41 Requested Font Not Available

- Check that correct font card or software font is installed.
- Check software setup.
- Defective font card.
- Defective system board.

42 Requested Font Not Available

- See error 41.

43 Font Card Error

- Font card was removed while the printer was turned on.
- Defective font card.
- Defective system board.

44 Font Card Error

- See error 43.

45 Downloaded Font Error

- Check software setup.
- Defective system board.

46 Download Character Error

- See error 45.

47 Language Error

- Unsupported card installed.
- If using Postscript, make sure card is installed and Postscript selected.
- Defective font card.
- Defective system board.

54 Serial Error

- Check serial communication settings on printer and computer.
- Defective serial cable.
- Defective serial port on computer.
- Defective system board.

55 Font Error

- See error 45.

89 Output Tray Full

- Clear paper from output tray.

- Check paper flag.
- Defective photo sensor.
- Defective cable.
- Defective system board.

900 System Board Failure

- Reseat options.
- Defective options.
- Defective system board.

910 Font Card Failure

- Reseat font card.
- Defective font card.
- Defective system board.

920 Fuser not up to Temperature

- Defective fuser.
- Defective low voltage power supply.
- Defective system cable 1.
- Defective fuser power cable.
- Defective system board.

921 Fuser not up to Temperature

- See 920 error.

922 Fuser not up to Temperature

- See 920 error.

923 Fuser Over Temperature

- See 920 error.

930 Mirror Motor not up to Speed

- Check cables between print head and system board.

- Defective print head.
- Defective system board.

931 Mirror Motor Speed Detect Error
- See error 930.

932 Mirror Motor Speed Detect Error
- See error 930.

940 Laser Beam Detect Failure
- See error 930.

941 Laser Beam Detect Failure
- See error 930.

950 System Board Failure
- See error 900.

960 Memory Error
- See error 900.

970 Fan not Turning
- Check cable between fan and system board.
- Defective fan.
- Defective system board.

980 System Board Failure
- See 900 error.

990 System Board Failure
- See 900 error.

Panasonic

E10 (Abnormal charge current or no +24V DC)

KX-P4450, P4450i, P4455

- Defective corona wire.
- Defective high voltage power supply.
- Defective logic PCB.

E12 (Discharge LED open or no +24V DC)

KX-P4450, P4450i, P4455

- Defective discharge LED.
- Defective driver PCB.
- Defective logic PCB.

E13 (Correct toner density not obtained)

KX-P4420, P4450, P4450i, P4455

- Defective developer unit.
- Defective hopper motor.
- Defective logic PCB.

E20 (Scanner motor speed has not stabilized)

All Printers

- Defective laser unit.
- Defective driver PCB.
- Defective logic PCB.

E21 (No apcend signal)

KX-P4450, P4450i

- Defective laser unit.
- Defective driver PCB.
- Defective logic PCB.
- Defective secondary power supply.

E25 (No apcend signal)

KX-P4420, P4450, P4450i, P4455

- Defective driver PCB.
- Defective logic PCB.
- Defective main motor.

E26 (Fan motor not on or no +24V DC)

KX-P4420, P4450, P4450i, P4455

- Check fan cable.
- Defective fan.
- Defective driver PCB.
- Defective logic PCB.

E30 (Fuser temperature over 446° F)

All Printers

- Defective fuser.
- Defective power supply.
- Defective logic PCB.
- Defective engine PCB (P4410/P4430).

E31 (Fuser temperature below 356° F)

All Printers

- Defective fuser.
- Defective power supply.
- Defective logic PCB.

E35

All Printers

- Defective laser unit.
- Defective logic PCB.

E36

KX-P4450

- Defective laser unit.
- Defective logic PCB.

E37

KX-P4450

- Defective laser unit.
- Defective logic PCB.

E38

KX-P4450

- Defective logic PCB.

E50 (DRAM failure)

All Printers

- Defective logic PCB.

E51 (Optional DRAM failure)

All Printers

- Defective memory expansion PCB.
- Defective logic PCB.

E52 (SRAM failure)

KX-P4450

- Defective logic PCB.

E53 (VRAM failure)

KX-P4450

- Defective logic PCB.

E54 (ROM check sum error)

All Printers
- Defective logic PCB.

E55 (ROM check sum error)

KX-P4450, P4455
- Defective logic PCB.

E56 (ROM check sum error)

All Printers
- Defective logic PCB.

E57 (Optional font card check sum error)

All Printers
- Defective font card.
- Defective logic PCB.

E60 (CPU error)

KX-P4410, P4420, P4430, P4450, P4450i
- Defective logic PCB.

E61 (CPU error)

KX-P4450, P4455
- Defective logic PCB.

E62 (Engine CPU error)

KX-P4410, P4430
- Defective engine PCB.

E62 (Abnormal dot resolution)

KX-P4450
- Defective logic PCB.

E63 (CPU error)

KX-P4450, P4455

- Defective logic PCB.

E64 (CPU error)

KX-P4450, P4455

- Defective logic PCB.

E65 (Abnormal horizontal/vertical converter)

KX-P4450

- Defective logic PCB.

E66 (Handshaking error)

KX-P4420

- Defective logic PCB.

E70 (Battery voltage incorrect)

KX-P4450, P4455

- Defective logic PCB.

E71 (EEPROM check error)

KX-P4410, P4420, P4430, P4450i

- Defective logic PCB.

Appendix B—Common Parts with Part Numbers

Hewlett-Packard

SX Engine (LaserJet II,IID,III,IIID)

RG1-0718	Paper Control PCA
RG1-0931	Paper Pickup Assembly
RG1-0932	Registration Assembly, II/III
RG1-1326	Registration Assembly, IID/IIID
RG1-1340	Lower Pickup Assembly
RG1-0939	Fusing Assembly (110V)
RG1-0945	Delivery Assembly
RG1-0936	High Voltage Power Supply
RG9-0319	AC Power Module (110V)
RG1-1394	DC Power Supply (110V), II/III
RG1-1310	DC Power Supply (110V), IID
RG1-2007	DC Power Supply (110V), IIID
RG0-0050	Laser Scanner Assembly
RG1-0710	DC Controller, II
RG1-1969	DC Controller, III
RG1-1278	DC Controller, IID
RG1-1970	DC Controller, IIID
RH7-1122	Upper Cooling Fan
RH7-1056	Lower Cooling Fan

RG1-0933	Transfer Corona Wire
RA1-3851	Paper Pickup Roller
RF1-1145	Separation Pad
RF1-2130	Ozone Filter
RG1-0966	Cleaning Wand
SG4-6212	Formatter PCA, II
33446-69001	Formatter PCA, IID
33497-67901	Formatter PCA, III/IIID

LX Engine (LaserJet IIp, IIp Plus, IIIp)

RG1-1792	MP Pickup Roller Assembly
RG1-1912	Separation Pad
RF1-2394	Input Feed Roller
RA1-7708	Delivery Roller
RG1-1791	Face Down Roller (Delivery) Assembly
RA1-7627	Transfer Roller
RG1-1777	Drum Drive Gear Assembly
RG1-1788	Fusing Assembly (110V)
RG1-1771	Scanner Motor Assembly
RG1-1604	Density PCA
RG1-1909	DC Power Supply (110V)
RG9-0696	High Voltage Power Supply
RG1-1933	DC Controller
RH7-1121	Cooling Fan
RH6-0010	Control Panel Assembly
RG6-1806	MP Tray Assembly

33471-60001	Formatter PCA, IIp
C2008-67901	Formatter PCA. IIp Plus
33481-67901	Formatter PCA, IIIp

EX Engine (LaserJet 4, 4 Plus, 5)

RB1-3477	Paper Pickup Roller, 4/4 Plus
RB1-7911	Paper Pickup Roller, 5
RB1-2127	MP Paper Pickup Roller, 4/4 Plus
RB1-2205	MP Paper Pickup Roller, 5
RF5-0343	MP Separation Pad
RB1-2632	LC Paper Pickup Roller, 4
RB1-2650	LC Paper Pickup Roller, 4 Plus
RB1-7983	LC Paper Pickup Roller, 5
RF5-0349	Transfer Roller
RB1-2133	Paper Out Sensor Flag
RG5-0886	Paper Output Assembly, 4/4 Plus
RG5-7911	Paper Output Assembly, 5
RG5-0454	Fusing Assembly (110V), 4
RG5-0879	Fusing Assembly (110V), 4 Plus/5
RG5-0451	Paper Feed Assembly, 4
RG5-0877	Paper Feed Assembly, 4 Plus
RG5-2195	Paper Feed Assembly, 5
RG5-2499	Power Supply (110V)
RG5-0513	High Voltage Power Supply, 4
RG5-0969	High Voltage Power Supply, 4 Plus/5
RG5-0449	Laser Scanner Assembly, 4

RG5-0903	Laser Scanner Assembly, 4 Plus/5
RG5-1078	DC Controller PCA, 4
RG5-0966	DC Controller PCA, 4 Plus/5
RH7-1143	Fan, 4
RH7-1177	Fan, 4 Plus
RH7-1178	Fan, 5
RH7-1151	Main Motor, 4
RH7-1301	Main Motor, 4 Plus/5
RG5-0514	Sensor PCA
RG5-0512	Paper Control PCA
C2002-67901	Formatter PCA, 4
C2038-67901	Formatter PCA, 4 Plus
C3919-67901	Formatter PCA, 5

BX Engine (LaserJet 4V)

RG5-1391	Paper Pickup Roller Assembly
RB1-1411	MP Paper Pickup Roller
RF5-0302	MP Separation Pad
RG5-1410	Transfer Roller
RG5-2248	Paper Guide Plate Assembly
RG5-1557	Fusing Assembly (110V)
RG5-0198	Face Down Delivery Assembly
RG5-1552	Front Door Assembly
RH7-1317	Fan
RH3-2150	Power Supply (110V)
RG5-2044	High Voltage Power Supply

RG5-2041	Laser Scanner Assembly
RG5-1559	DC Controller PCA
C3143-67901	Formatter PCA

NX Engine (LaserJet IIISi, 4Si)

RF5-0041	Paper Feed/Separation Roller
RG5-0141	Transfer Roller
RB1-0818	Transfer Clip
RG5-0161	Registration Assembly
RG5-0046	Fusing Assembly (110V)
RG5-0381	Job Offset Assembly
RG5-0025	Paper Input Unit (PIU)
RG5-0067	Delivery Cover Assembly
RG5-0040	Main Motor Drive Assembly
RG5-0042	Main Motor PCA
RG5-0095	AC Power Module (110V), IIISi
RG5-0166	AC Power Module (110V), 4Si
RG5-0085	DC Power Supply (110V), IIISi
RG5-0168	DC Power Supply (110V), 4Si
RG5-0076	High Voltage Power Supply, IIISi
RG5-0170	High Voltage Power Supply, 4Si
RG5-0021	Laser Scanner Assembly, IIISi
RG5-0153	Laser Scanner Assembly, 4Si
RG5-0095	DC Controller, IIISi
RG5-0842	DC Controller, 4Si
33491-60143	Formatter PCA (S/N £ 3199), IIISi

33491-60160	Formatter PCA (S/N ³ 3200), IIISi
C2009-69001	Formatter PCA, 4Si

PX Engine (LaserJet 4L,4P)

RB1-3029	Paper Pickup D-Roller, 4L
RB1-3368	Paper Pickup D-Roller, 4P
RG5-0668	Paper Pickup Assembly, 4L
RG5-0796	Paper Pickup Assembly, 4P
RF5-0596	Transfer Roller
RF5-0601	Input Sensor Arm
RG5-0676	Fusing Assembly (110V)
RG5-0765	Main Motor Assembly
RG5-0711	Top Oblique Roller Assembly
RG5-0669	Front Oblique Roller Assembly
RG5-0753	DC Controller PCA (110V), 4L
RG5-0822	DC Controller PCA (110V), 4P
RG5-0662	Laser Scanner Assembly, 4L
RG5-0800	Laser Scanner Assembly, 4P
C2004-69001	Formatter PCA, 4L
C2016-69001	Formatter PCA, 4ML
C2006-69001	Formatter PCA, 4P
C2041-69001	Formatter PCA, 4MP

VX Engine (LaserJet 5P,6P)

RB1-2205	Tray 1 Pickup Roller
RF5-0343	Tray 1 Separation Pad
RB1-6332	Tray 2 Pickup Roller

RG9-1082	Tray 1 Pickup Assembly, 5P
RG5-2791	Tray 1 Pickup Assembly, 6P
RG9-1692	Tray 2 Pickup Assembly, 5P
RG9-2796	Tray 2 Pickup Assembly, 6P
RB1-6006	Paper Input Sensor Arm
RF5-1290	Transfer Roller Assembly, 5P
RF5-0596	Transfer Roller Assembly, 6P
RG5-1698	Top Oblique Roller Assembly
RF5-1283	Static Charge Eliminator
RG5-1700	Fusing Assembly (110V), 5P
RG5-4110	Fusing Assembly (110V), 6P
RG5-1799	Main Motor Assembly, 5P
RG5-2786	Main Motor Assembly, 6P
RG5-1780	Laser Scanner Assembly, 5P
RG5-2848	Laser Scanner Assembly, 6P
RG5-1798	DC Controller PCA (110V), 5P
RG5-2826	DC Controller PCA (110V), 6P
C3151-69001	Formatter PCA, 5P
C3891-69001	Formatter PCA, 6P

AX Engine (LaserJet 5L, 6L, 3100, 3150)

RG5-1951	Paper Pickup Roller Assembly, 5L
RG5-3486	Paper Pickup Roller Assembly, 6L/3100/3150
RY7-5077	Separation Pad Kit
RF5-1534	Transfer Roller
RF5-1516	Pressure Roller, 5L

RF5-2364   Pressure Roller, 6L/3100/3150

RG5-1964   Fixing Assembly (110V), 5L

RG5-3459   Fixing Assembly (110V), 6L

RG5-4678   Fixing Assembly (110V), 3100/3150

RG5-2023   DC Controller PCA (110V), 5L

RG5-3506   DC Controller PCA (110V), 6L

RG5-2000   Laser Scanner Assembly, 5L

RG5-3494   Laser Scanner Assembly, 6L

C3948-60001   LIU Assembly, 3100/3150

C3942-67902   Formatter Assembly, 5L

C3991-60001   Formatter Assembly, 6L

WX Engine (LaserJet 5Si, 5Si Mopier, 8000)

RF5-1835   Tray 2 & 3 Paper Pickup Roller

RF5-1834   Feed Separation Roller

RG5-1880   Tray 1 Pickup Assembly

RG5-1852   Tray 2 & 3 Pickup Assembly

RB1-6730   Tray 1 Feed Roller

RF5-1455   Tray 1 Separation Pad

RG5-1887   Transfer Roller Assembly

RG5-4447   Fusing Assembly (110V)

RG5-1833   Registration Assembly

RG5-1874   Face Down Delivery Assembly

RG5-1844   DC Controller PCA

RG5-1895   Laser Scanner Assembly

22X Engine (LaserJet 1100, 3200)

RB2-4026	Paper Pickup Roller
RF5-2886	Separation Pad Arm
RY7-5050	Subpad Kit
RG5-4657	Transfer Roller
RF5-2823	Lower Pressure Roller
RG5-4589	Fuser Assembly (110V)

52X Engine (LaserJet 4000, 4050)

RF5-2490	Feed Separation Roller
RG5-2655	Tray 1 Pickup Assembly
RG5-3718	Tray 1 Pickup Roller
RG5-4283	Transfer Roller
RG5-2661	Fusing Assembly (110V)
RG5-2652	Registration Assembly
RG5-3693	Engine Control Board (110V)
RG5-2641	Laser Scanner Assembly
C4119-67902	Coupler Kit
C4118-67908	Formatter PCA, 4000
C4251-67909	Formatter PCA, 4050

62X Engine (LaserJet 5000)

RB2-1820	Tray 1 Pickup Roller
RB2-1821	Tray 2 & 3 Pickup Roller
RF5-3439	Tray 1 Separation Pad
RG9-1485	Tray 2 Separation Pad
RG5-3579	Transfer Roller

RG5-5455	Fuser Assembly (110V)
RH3-2224	Power Supply (110V)
RG5-3542	Delivery Assembly
RG5-3517	DC Controller PCA

IBM/Lexmark

LaserPrinter 4019, 4029

1039105	Pickup "D" Roller
1383387	Transfer Corona Assembly
1383998	Fan Assembly
1381889	Fuser Assembly (110V), 4019
1381889	Fuser Assembly (110V), 4029 ver. 01x
1383522	Fuser Assembly (110V), 4029 ver. 02x, 03x, 04x
1039488	System Cable #1, 4019
99A1119	System Cable #1, 4029

APPENDIX C—VENDORS

Parts Now!

3517 W. Beltline Hwy.

Madison, WI 53713

Tel: 800-886-6688

Fax: 608-276-9593

Web: www.partsnow.com

Email: salessupport@partsnowllc.com

Pre-Owned Electronics

125 Middlesex Turnpike

Bedford, MA 01730

Tel: 800-274-5343

Fax: 781-778-4848

Web: www.preowned.com

Email: sales@preowned.com

The Printer Works

3481 Arden Rd.

Hayward, CA 94545

Tel: 800-225-6116

Fax: 510-786-0589

Web: www.printerworks.com

Email: info@printerworks.com

MCM, an In One company

650 Congress Park Drive

Centerville, OH 45459

Tel: 800-543-4330

Fax: 800-765-6960

Web: mcm.newark.com

Depot America, Inc.

1495 Highway 34 South

Farmingdale, NJ 07727

Tel: 866-326-7337

Fax: 732-919-7747

Web: www.depot-america.com

Email: sales@depot-america.com

0-595-34305-8

www.ingramcontent.com/pod-product-compliance
Lightning Source LLC
Chambersburg PA
CBHW051247050326
40689CB00007B/1096